Messerschmitt Bf 109
AT WAR

Messerschmitt
Bf109
AT WAR

Armand van Ishoven

LONDON
IAN ALLAN LTD

Contents

To Elza . . .
who like hundreds of thousands
of mothers feared for her son during the
long years of the Second World War.

First published 1977

ISBN 0 7110 0770 5

Designed by David J Kingston

© Armand van Ishoven, 1977

Published by Ian Allan Ltd, Shepperton, Surrey,
and printed in the United Kingdom by
Ian Allan Printing Ltd.

Glossary

Luftwaffe ranks
The following table is simply a general comparison level of rank with its contemporary Royal Air Force equivalent. Several German ranks, in fact, had no direct equivalent in the British service.

Flieger – Aircraftman 2 (AC2)
Gefreiter – Aircraftmen 1 (AC1)
Obergefreiter – Leading Aircraftman (LAC)
Hauptgefreiter – Corporal
Unteroffizier/Unterfeldwebel – Sergeant
Feldwebel – Flight Sergeant
Oberfeldwebel/Stabsfeldwebel – Warrant Officer
Leutnant – Pilot Officer
Oberleutnant – Flying Officer
Hauptmann – Flight Lieutenant
Major – Squadron Leader
Oberstleutnant – Wing Commander
Oberst – Group Captain
Generalmajor – Air Commodore
Generalleutnant – Air Vice-Marshal
General der Flieger – Air Marshal
Generaloberst/Generalfeldmarschall – Air Chief Marshal
Reichsmarschall – Marshal of the RAF

Luftwaffe formations
Rotte/Deckungsrotte – Two fighters working as a fighting pair.
Schwarm – Two *Rotte*
Kette – Unit of three or four fighters
Staffel – 10 to 12 aircraft; nearest equivalent to RAF squadron
Gruppe – Three, occasionally four *Staffeln*

Geschwader – Literally 'Squadron'; comprised of three *Gruppen* usually.
Alarmstaffel – Fighter defence Flight.
Jagdstaffel – Fighter *staffel*
Nachtjagdstaffel – Night fighter *staffel*
Kunstflugstaffel – Aerobatic team, varying in numbers.

General terms
Alarmstart – Equivalent to RAF 'scramble' take-off.
Dicke Autos – Luftwaffe slang for four-engined Allied bombers
Flak – Anti-aircraft; from *Fliegerabwehrkanone*
Fl. Kp – *Fliegerkompagnie;* 'squadron' in Swiss flying services
Flugleitung – Airfield control section
Gefechtsstand – Command post/operational HQ
Hals-und Beinbruch – Literally 'May you break your neck and legs' – a traditional 'Good Luck' greeting by German fliers prior to a take-off; dates from World War I
Kriegsberichter – War correspondents
Pauke – Night fighter's equivalent of RAF's 'Tally Ho', signifying 'Attack!'
Prüfleiter – Head Technical Inspector
Rottenflieger – Wing man; also *Rottenkamerad/Kaczmarek;* same as RAF's 'No. 2'.
Viktor – Equivalent of RAF's 'Roger'; radio code for 'Yes, OK, understood' et al.
Wachtmeister – Technical Sergeant
Wart – General nickname for ground crew man; equivalent to RAF 'Erk'; also 'Black Man' from black overalls usually worn.
Werkstattszüge – Mobile workshops

Introduction

Schwarm. How a fighting foursome of Bf 109s looked to a potential opponent . . .

During 1939 to 1945 many thousands of the world's youth fought each other in small, fast, agile single-engined aircraft which offered only minimal protection against an enemy's fire, for they were encased in thin aluminium sheeting incapable of stopping a bullet. Carrying large amounts of highly inflammable fuel, such aircraft were apt to burst into searing flames or simply explode if hit. One such aircraft was the Messerschmitt Bf 109.

This book is in no way an attempt to record the full history of the Bf 109's technical development or its operational use. Very fine volumes of this nature have already been published, and this book is designed to complement them. Some of the accounts herein first appeared in German publications during the war, hence the reader should be warned that some of them may have been coloured for propaganda and/or ideological reasons. Nevertheless, it was considered useful to include a few such accounts as they were written by first-hand witnesses shortly after the action described.

Naturally, one cannot disassociate the aircraft from its designer, Professor Willy Messerschmitt. The world has yet to see

another engineer-designer produce an aircraft of which no less than 33,000 were actually built, and many of them in his own factory. Yet Messerschmitt's path to success was no bed of roses, anymore than was the career of his design, the Bf 109.

The first-ever design by young Willy Messerschmitt – he was 22 years old then – was a failure. A tail-less glider, the S9, it made its first flight on 7 May, 1921 and proved to be dangerously unstable. Considerable modification failed to make it safe to fly. When he entered two powered gliders of his own design in his first contest – the annual Rhön gliding competition, 15 to 31 August, 1924 – he met further setbacks. One of these, the S16a 'Bubi', was a total write-off after its propeller flew apart in flight; while the other, the S16b 'Betti', had to make an emergency landing when a drive chain broke. His first sports machine, the two-seat, high-wing M17, he entered in another contest, the Zugspitzflug of 31 January, 1925, carrying competition number 3. It was the only one of 13 contestants which failed to leave Schleissheim airfield, as heavy turbulence caused by the Föhn pushed it back on the ground just after take-

off, tipping it on its nose! When, on 16 May, 1925, Messerschmitt flew for the first time in his life in one of his own designs, as a passenger in an M17, the aircraft hit some high tension wires on 'finals' at Bamberg airfield and crashed, sending Messerschmitt and his pilot, Seywald, to hospital.

The most important sports flying event in Germany in 1927 was the Sachsenflug, held at the Leipzig-Mockau airfield from 30 August till 5 September. Messerschmitt designed his M19 especially for this contest and two examples were built. When the round flight of over 450km came on Sunday, 4 September the M19, D-1221, flown by Theo Croneiss, had to make an emergency landing near Warchau, Borna, having run out of fuel. The second machine, D-1206, flown by Eberhard von Conta, was written off when it had to 'land' in a forest near Bautzen, as its Bristol Cherub II engine was malfunctioning. Yet both aircraft won the Sachsenflug and brought home some 60,000 Reichmarks in prize money! Messerschmitt had so cleverly tailored the M19 – his first-ever low wing design – to the rules of the competition that it had received the handicap 'Infinite' and had thereby become the winner before even participating! Less than three weeks later, on 22 September, D-1177, one of the earliest examples of his successful four-seater airliner, the M18a, crashed at Schwarza in Germany, killing its pilot Hellmuth Schnabel of the

Deutsche Verkehrsflug AG and two passengers, although through no fault of the aircraft. The first prototype of the M20 airliner – the first Messerschmitt design to be ordered by the Deutsche Lufthansa – crashed on its first flight from Augsburg airfield on 26 February, 1928, killing its pilot Dipl Ing Hans Hackmack, a test pilot on temporary leave from Lufthansa, when he tried to jump from the aircraft after some fabric on the left wing's upper surface came loose. Hackmack had previously reached a height – then a record – of 303metres in August 1923, at the Rhön contest, flying a Harth-Messerschmitt S14 glider.

On behalf of the engine manufacturers Siemens and Halske AG, two pilots, Dr Georg Pasewaldt and Dipl Ing J von Berg, undertook a two-months demonstration tour through southern Europe with D-1229, a BFW U-12 'Flamingo', a type which was then BFW's bread-and-butter machine. Starting on 1 July, 1929, the tour successfully demonstrated the aircraft at Vienna-Aspern, Graz-Thalerhof, Budapest, Belgrade, Bucharest, Gorno, Sofia, Thessaloniki, Athens, Brindisi, Naples, Rome, Pisa, Milan, St Raphael and Marseilles, but then the plane crashed at Barcelona. On 14 October, 1930 the first military aircraft produced by Messerschmitt's firm BFW (Bayerische Flugzeugwerke) – the M22 twin-engined biplane bomber, disguised as a 'mail carrier' –

crashed while on a test flight; killing its pilot Eberhardt Mohnike, a WW1 fighter pilot who had served with Jasta II and had obtained nine victories. The cause was again failure of one of the three-blade propellers, which flew apart in mid-air. On 6 October that year, D-1930, one of the Lufthansa's M20b aircraft, crashed on a Reichswehr firing range while about to land at Dresden airfield during the regular service between Berlin-Dresden-Prague-Vienna. All aboard – pilot Erich Pust, wireless operator Hermann Lange, five male passengers and the wife of Lufthansa's representative in Sofia – were killed. To add to the dismal chain of events, D-1928, another Lufthansa M20, crashed at Rietschen, in Silesia, on 14 April, 1931 while on a charter flight, killing its pilot Adolf Schirmer and flight mechanic Ulrich Bischoff, though only slightly bruising some of the passengers, all of whom were Reichswehr officers. The effective result of all these crashes was that Lufthansa refused to accept any more M20s. Nothing now could prevent Messerschmitt's company, BFW, going bankrupt on 1 June, 1931.

Hardly three months later came the news that D-1812, an M18d owned by the Deutsche Verkehrsflug AG but operated by the Munich Photogrammetrie GmbH firm, had crashed on 16 September near Ljungbyhed, Sweden during some photo survey work. The machine had shed a wing when the pilot, Johann Wirtz, had attempted to dive through

Left: Lufthansa mechanics servicing the 700hp BMW VIu engine of D-2005, 'Odenwald' (Wk Nr 549, later re-registered as D-UNAH); one of the M-20bs which served Lufthansa faithfully for many years. Note how a cowling panel served as a servicing platform. During WW2, six M-20bs and two M-20as continued to be flown by Lufthansa, and the last remaining pair – a M-20a and a M-20b – were destroyed in 1943 while on charter to the Luftwaffe./ *Lufthansa*

Below: D-2307, the M-29 in which Fritz Morzik intended to participate in the 3rd Challenge de Tourisme International, after landing at Brunswick on 8 August, 1932 to learn that his friend Kreutzkamp had crashed in another M-29. The type was immediately grounded by the DVL. Morzik became a 'Generalmajor' during the war, and was the Luftwaffe's last Chief of Wehrmacht Air Transport./ *F Morzik*

a hole in the overcast. The man sent to investigate the accident was Dipl Ing Heinrich Hertel of the Adlershof Research Facility (DVL) for Aviation; he was later to become Ernst Heinkel's chief of development and as such responsible for the Heinkel He 112b, the Messerschmitt Bf 109's most serious competitor. In 1932 Messerschmitt developed an aircraft especially for the Challenge de Tourisme International, the European aircraft rally. D-2308, one of four racing M29 low-wing two-seaters that were to take part, crashed on 8 August, a few days before the contest, killing its pilot Fridolin Kreutzkamp, a flying instructor. The following day another M29 failed in the air, killing its flight mechanic Starchinsky, though the pilot Reinhold Poss parachuted to safety. Immediately the M29 was banned from flying by the DVL and therefore from participating in the event for which it had been particularly designed. In 1934 Messerschmitt again designed a machine for this same international rally, the M37, later to become famous as the Bf 108 'Taifun'. Ill-luck continued to dog his efforts, and a few days before the contest, on 27 July, 1934 the first prototype, D-IBUM, crashed near Augsburg, killing its pilot Freiherr Wolf von Dungern, an official with the German Ministry of Aviation. Only feverishly executed

Below: How Ernst Udet saw the rivalry between Willy Messerschmitt (l) and Ernst Heinkel (r). On 6 June, 1938, Udet flew the Heinkel He 100V-2 to better the 100km closed circuit landplane speed record of 634.73 km hr; after which both designers tried to capture the absolute world speed record.

Bottom: Presentation of D-IONO, a Bf 108 'Taifun', on the airfield at Campo dos Affonsos, near Rio de Janeiro, Brazil on 29 May, 1936. It crossed the Atlantic aboard the Zeppelin LZ 129 – the ill-fated 'Hindenburg'./ *Dipl Ing Fuchs*

modifications permitted the other Bf 108 aircraft to take part in the rally. Ultimately it became one of Messerschmitt's most outstanding designs.

Even when the Bf 109 finally appeared, the dispiriting saga of accidents and setbacks did not cease. In the summer of 1935, D-IABI, the first Bf 109 prototype, was flown from the Augsburg factory to the E-Stelle (Erprobungs-Stelle – testing centre) at Rechlin to be tested by Luftwaffe experts, but its undercarriage gave way during landing. This was a bad start for a fighter which already appeared to stand little chance of being ordered in quantity for the Luftwaffe, though ultimately it was put into series production. The first of the three prototypes – Bf 109 V3 D-IOQY, WN 760 – to be sent to Spain for operational evaluation by the Legion Condor crashed on take-off for its first flight in Spain, from Seville airfield on 10 December 1936. The normal teething troubles associated with any new type of aircraft taken into service, combined with the Bf 109's novel flying characteristics, began to take their toll. The second of the three prototypes sent to Spain – Bf 109 V4, D-IALY, *Werke – Nummer 878* – was damaged when landing at Villa del Prado from its first operational mission on 20 January 1937. Its tail-wheel failed to extend and the rudder was damaged in the ensuing landing. Leutnant Hannes Trautloft, the pilot of this first-ever combat sortie for a Bf 109, decided to have the tail wheel locked down.

The first Bf 109B-2 to be licence-built by the Gerhard Fieseler Werke GmbH at Kassel (*WN* 3001) made a belly-landing on 21 January, 1937; the accident report stated that the undercarriage would not lower. A month later, on 26 February, the first Bf 109 of the B-series, D-IPSA, *WN* 1001, crashed near

Augsburg after being side-slipped too steeply, killing its pilot. On 7 April, D-IIBA (*WN* 808) of the E'Stelle, Rechlin, belly-landed with a jammed undercarriage; on 5 August *WN* 325 of Lehrgeschwader II, Barth, collided with another aircraft during combat formation training, though its pilot baled out safely; and on 8 September *WN* 1034 crashed at Felgentreu. The pilot of *WN* 1034, Oberleutnant Pantke, had never flown a Bf 109 at altitude and was unfamiliar with the oxygen equipment; he lost consciousness, crashed, and was killed.

When in February 1937 the first Bf 109 B-1s were delivered to II./JG 132 'Richthofen' at Jüterbog-Damm, there was a spate of unexplained fatalities. It was only when on 29 May, 1938, Dr Ing Hermann Wurster was performing terminal-velocity dives that the reason for these accidents became clear. While he was recovering from a dive one half of the stabiliser suddenly flew off. He managed to bring back the crippled 109 to base where

Top: At the official opening of the new Budapest-Budaörs airfield in Hungary on 20 June, 1937, eight Bf 109Bs gave the new fighter its debut to non-German audiences.

Above: Bf 109E of Lt Miessfeldt, of 9./JG 2, which hit some birch trees on take-off from Signy-le-Petit, near Sedan, 1940. Note how the cockpit section survived virtually intact./R Rothenfelder

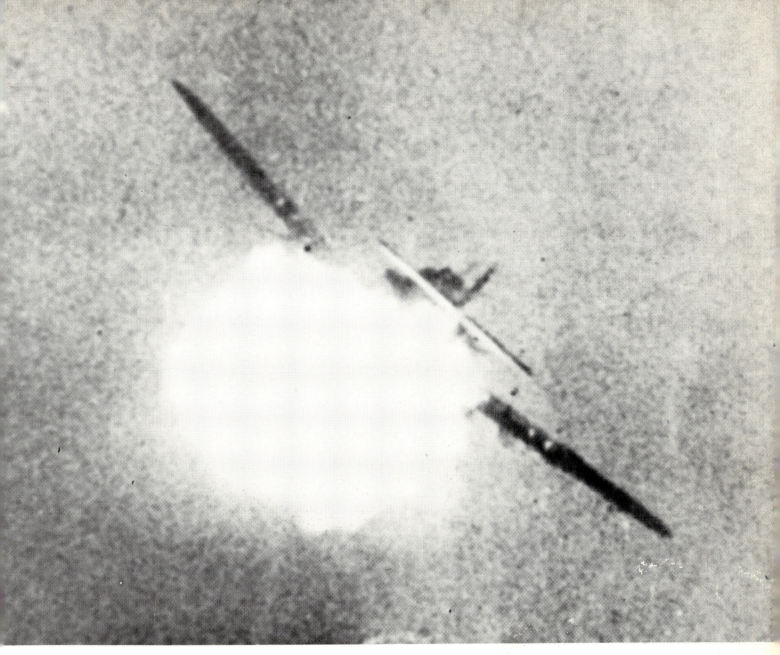

it was found that the front attachment fitting of the stabiliser had given way. Several other machines then revealed cracks at the same spot.

The pilot of *WN* 1038 of II/JG 132, Jüterbog-Damm, inadvertently feathered its propeller after take-off on 3 March, 1938, thereby cutting the engine. Trying to regain the airfield, he stalled, crashed and was killed. Three weeks later, on 31 March, the pilot of *WN* 539 of I/JG 234 Köln tried a steep turn after taking off from Göttingen airfield for a ferry flight to Köln-Ostheim; the Bf 109 stalled and killed him.

The Bf 109's debut outside Germany was equally chequered. For the official opening of the new Budapest-Budaörs airfield in Hungary a large aviation display was organised on 20 June, 1937. The Luftwaffe decided to send a *Kunstflugstaffel* (aerobatics team) of nine Bf 109s. Pilots from various fighter units were selected and ordered to Bad Aibling for training. The team leader was Major von Janson from the RLM; leader of the left *Kette*, or sub-Flight, was Oberleutnant Hannes Trautloft; and leader of the right *Kette* was Oberleutnant Strümpel. Preliminary training proved impossible because of bad weather conditions, and when the nine Bf 109s took off at Budapest for their unrehearsed display Strümpel's aircraft lost its canopy, leaving eight machines to perform, in asymmetrical formation. Because of his inexperience in formation aerobatics, Major von Janson forgot to allow for the very strong wind that day, and the flying display was flown practically out of sight of the spectators. A final loop, started with too little speed, then scattered the eight Messerschmitts all over the sky. That evening the pilots, without their *Staffelkapitän*, tried to drown their sorrows in a Budapest bar where the speciality of the *Bardamen*, or bar ladies, was distributing false beards to customers. Next day eight of the nine Bf 109s were flown from Budapest to Bad Aibling by bearded pilots.

Below: FIRST TO SPAIN.
D-IOQY, Bf 109 V3 (Wk Nr
760), the first example to fly
in Spain, in late 1936, was
damaged on its first landing
there on 11 December, 1936.
Seen here over the Wertach,
a tributary of the River Lech,
west of Augsburg airfield.

Bottom right: Inside the
Projektbüro, where such
famous aircraft as the Bf
108, Bf 109 and Bf 110 were
'born'. Far left is Dipl Ing
Robert Lusser, and next to
him Dipl Ing Woldemar
Voigt of Me 262 fame.
Photograph taken in 1939.

Born in Bavaria

D-IOQY

Augsburg dates from 15 BC, when a settlement was founded in that part of Bavaria by the Romans, who bestowed upon it the name Augusta Vindelicorum, in honour of Emperor Augustus. It was well situated. Many roads coming from the Alpine passes converged there and crossed an important east-west road. In the days of Tacitus the settlement had already become an important trading centre, and during Augsburg's most splendid period of history – the 15th, 16th and early 17th centuries – the names of some of its most prominent merchants, like Fugger and Welser, became world-famous. Alongside the road leading to Landsberg in the south, near Haunstetten, lay the site of the airfield where the Bayerische Rumpler Werke AG built Rumpler machines during the 1914-18 war. And it was there that the Bf 109 story started. Indeed, it was in Augsburg that, on 30 July, 1926, the Bayerische Flugzeugwerke AG (BFW) was incorporated and established itself in the factory of the former Rumperwerke on Augsburg-Haunstetten airfield, using the machinery of the Udet-Flugzeugbau GmbH. At the head of BFW was Willy Messerschmitt. Bankruptcy proceedings had been started against the concern at the Augsburg court on 1 June, 1931, but an agreement had been reached between all creditors at a meeting in December 1932, and on 1 May, 1933 the BFW AG was able to start a new career.

On 1 November, 1933 Dipl Ing Robert Lusser joined BFW as head of the project office that took care of aero-dynamics and configuration design of new projects. His salary was 800 Reichmarks per month, augmented by RM 0.50 per horsepower of every aircraft delivered to a customer! During the first post-World War I Deutschlandflug (an air rally around Germany) in 1925 Lusser became acquainted with Hans Klemm, chief designer in the aircraft building department

of the Daimler Motor company at Sindelfingen. He immediately persuaded Klemm to take him into his employ and to teach him the intricacies of aircraft design. When Klemm founded his own firm, Klemm Flugzeugbau GmbH, at Böblingen in the following year, Lusser remained with him, becoming a director of the company and taking part in various design projects. The first such design was the L25 low-wing, two-seater sports aircraft, and later Lusser was involved in most other Klemm machines, including the Klemm Kl-31 and Kl 32, low-wing, three- and four-seater tourers. In 1932 he left Klemm to join the Ernst Heinkel Flugzeugwerke GmbH at Warnemünde, where he became chief of the design department for sports aircraft. In this capacity he designed the Heinkel He 71, a single-seat development of the fast He 64 which had been designed by the twin brothers, Siegfried and Walter Günter.

On 20 October, 1933, just nine months after Adolf Hitler came to power in Germany, Hermann Göring, who had been Minister of the Reich for Aviation since 1 May that year, expressed the hope that BFW would design a fast fighter. He did so in a highly confidential letter to Theo Croneiss, another ex-World War I fighter pilot, whom Göring had ordered to liquidate his Deutsche Verkehrflug AG, Lufthansa's only competitor, after which Göring asked him to join Messerschmitt in reorganising and rebuilding the BFW company.

'I dare expect of your energy', wrote Göring, 'that you will immediately and passionately build up an aircraft firm which, I hope, will soon bring out a first-class airliner. Equally important, however, is the development of a lightning-fast courier aircraft (*blitzschnelles Kurierflugzeug*) which needs only to be a single seater . . . Furthermore, I ask you to destroy this letter after reading, for reasons that are clear to you.

With Heil Hitler and best wishes.'

GÖRING

Naturally, Göring could not specifically say, even in a 'to be destroyed' confidential letter, that he expected Messerschmitt to design a military fighter. Nevertheless, both Croneiss and Messerschmitt were in no doubt as to what was meant by a *blitzschnelles Kurierflugzeug*.

A few weeks later, early in 1934, the C-Amt (Technical Office) of Göring's Ministry issued a requirement for a single-seat, all-metal monoplane fighter, based on a concept of the staff of the still-secret Luftwaffe, to supersede the Luftwaffe's first-generation biplane fighters. This requirement was issued to selected aircraft manufacturers, including Focke-Wulf, Ernst Heinkel and Arado – but *not to BFW*.

The omission was directly attributable to Göring's deputy, Erhard Milch, one of Lufthansa's directors and, since the various M20 accidents, Messerschmitt's chief detractor. After prolonged arguments the requirement for a new fighter was finally, if reluctantly, issued to BFW, though it was made clear to Messerschmitt that any development contract was not likely to be followed by a series production order. Messerschmitt lost no time in starting the design of a fighter as specified.

Various writers in the past have claimed that the Bf 109 was designed by Willy Messerschmitt and Oberingenieur Walter Rethel. In late 1975, from Bad Wörishofen, Rethel himself wrote to the author that, the types Bf 108 and Bf 109 originated in 1934. 'I came from the Arado works and joined Messerschmitt AG as chief of the design department that drew the blueprints needed actually to build the aircraft in March 1938.' In fact, when the design of the Bf 109 was initiated in March 1934, it drew heavily on the experience gained from designing the all-metal four-seater M37 (later titled Bf 108), design of which had started some seven months earlier, and the first flight of which was only three months away. Much of the work was done by Robert Lusser and his office.

Also working on the Bf 109 project was Richard Bauer, chief design engineer. Responsible for actual construction of the first prototype was Hubert Bauer, workshop manager and head of the experimental construction department. Born 20 March, 1902, Bauer had joined the Junkers Works at Dessau in 1925 as a jig designer, before going to work for Messerschmitt in 1929. He was later to become a specialist in the series production of aircraft and was still with Messerschmitt when, after World War 2, licence-construction of F-104G Starfighters was taken in hand.

Collaboration between Messerschmitt and Lusser was not always easy, as witness this note sent by Lusser to Messerschmitt when the former returned from his winter vacation in early 1935:

'After returning from my vacation I was told that you have raised extremely grave reproaches against Herr von Chlingensperg and against the Projektbüro (Lusser's department) I take this opportunity to note down also those items that have, since the Europarundflug, sometimes caused grave altercations between yourself and the Projektbüro.

Below: 'Gefolgschaftsabend' – an evening reunion of BFW staff at Augsburg in 1937. Bottom left, wearing spectacles, is Robert Lusser; to his right Kurt Tank of Fw 190 fame. At top is Hubert Bauer, next to Willy Stör, holding paper. Just behind Lusser is Erwin Aichele, famed for his sport-flying exploits with BFW or Messerschmitt aircraft.

Bottom: Willy Messerschmitt (left) with the manager of the experimental workshop Hubert Bauer, admiring models of BFW-designed aircraft in the professor's office.

1 *Performance calculations Me 109*
In mid-November 1934 you announced that according to your calculations the climbing performance of the Me 109 had been given as some two minutes (= 25%) too favourable, and that you had requested Herr Urban to check the calculations independently of the Projektbüro. After a day and a half you came to me, very excited, and declared that your fears had been proved true, and that the firm has been much harmed through our mistake. However, it became clear that Herr Urban had yet to finish his calculations; when these were completed, a climbing time was determined which was even better than that calculated and guaranteed by us. . . .

2 *Diving speed:*
At the end of October the diving speed of the Me 109 had to be calculated. The result of our calculation seemed to be impossibly high to you, and you ordered Herr Kraus to check our calculations again. The result was that Herr Kraus indicated our calculations though novel in method were correct.

3 *The profile problem:*
In mid-November you reproached us on the occasion of the choice of a wing profile for the Me 109, saying we had not taken into consideration the profile of the M29. As in previous cases, I explained to you that the M29 profile was not only not better, but even markedly worse than the American profile that is used by us. Yet, to date, you have not acknowledged this clear proof, and continue to think of using the M29 profile again.

4 *Me 109 drag measurements. Interference.*
In early December thorough drag measurements and calculations were made for the Me 109. Due to measuring differences between the two wind tunnels at Göttingen there was some uncertainty in the results, which could, however, have been cleared up had we limited our measurements to the one wind tunnel. During these (last) 14 days you have, you say, not slept for nights on end! My constant efforts to calm you down . . . were totally without result. On the other hand you have reproached me daily that I treated these questions much too lightly, and that I resisted your efforts to reach the ultimate in speed. The final calculations and considerations proved that all your calculations were wrong!'

Lusser also touched on other subjects, such as the weight of the Bf 110's wing spar, the length of the Bf 110's fuselage, and impossible deadlines. He ended the note by saying:

'Nobody would be happier than I if the candid airing of these various items leads to clearing the (present) atmosphere, which is in the interests chiefly of yourself and the BFW.'

Three views depicting the unique way in which the Bf 109s rear fuselage was built up. Alternate sheets of the skin covering were drawn and bent to form Z-section flanges on the inside of the fuselage. The sheets were further joggled to make flush skin laps possible. These were clamped in jigs and joined by un-flanged sheets alternately, then rivetted.

At the end of May 1935 – not September, as widely stated – and barely 15 months after Messerschmitt had initiated its design, the all-silver D-IABI, the first-ever Bf 109, stood ready for its first flight on Augsburg-Haunstetten airfield. *Flugkapitän* Hans Knoetzsch, a 27-years old test pilot, was standing by. Nicknamed 'Bubi' by all, Knoetzsch had only joined BFW the previous year. After a spell as a bank clerk in Berlin, he had been selected for a free course of flying tuition by the Ring der Flieger in 1924 while he was still too young. Working at the Berlin-Staaken airfield office of the Sportflug until he could start learning to fly in 1925, he then obtained his seaplane, glider and blind-flying ratings. In 1929-30 he was the works-pilot with Hanns Klemm Flugzeugbau GmbH, where Robert Lusser was also working at that time. From 1930-34 he was pilot and scientific assistant at the German Aviation Research Institute at Berlin-Adlershof, then he joined Messerschmitt's BFW as chief pilot in 1934. Two years later he was to leave BFW to become Fieseler's chief pilot.

On this May day, however, he was to make the first test flight of the world's most advanced fighter. Donning the white gloves without which he never flew, he climbed into the narrow cockpit, closed the canopy and started the Rolls-Royce Kestrel engine. After a brief check of the engine, Knoetzsch made several ground runs across the airfield. Then – the moment of truth. Positioning himself at the end of the airfield, he made a final check of the engine and took off. The prototype Bf 109 had no automatic undercarriage retraction mechanism, so he had to wind the wheels up manually. On the ground Messerschmitt and his staff anxiously followed every movement of D-IABI.

Knoetzsch stayed airborne for 20 minutes, making several circuits of the airfield, then came in to land. When he opened the canopy, his smiling face told everyone concerned that the Bf 109 possessed perfect handling qualities the Bf 109 possessed perfect handling qualities. The Bf 109 was born – six months before the first Hawker Hurricane and 10 months before the first Supermarine Spitfire.

Below: Dipl Ing Walter Rethel, the man usually credited with the design of the Bf 109, but who did not join Messerschmitt until March 1938 when the Bf 109 had already been in production for over a year. Seen here (left) with Willy Messerschmitt in 1943./ *Dipl Ing W Rethel*

Left: PROTOTYPE, D-IABI. On arrival at Rechlin after its first ferry flight from Augsberg, via Leipzig, D-IABI's undercarriage collapsed.

Below: A sight which had seemed impossible in 1934, but first became a reality in 1936 – series production at Messerschmitt's works. A wartime Bf 109G assembly line; giving an excellent 'inside' view of the much-criticised Bf 109 undercarriage attachments and assembly./*MBB GmbH*

The Designer Speaks

On Monday, 22 November, 1937, Adolf Hitler visited Augsburg, where the Bf 109 was demonstrated to him. From left; Betriebsführer (Works Manager) Theo Croneiss; Hitler; Rayan Kokothaki, who succeeded Croneiss when the latter died in 1942; Karl Wahl, Gauleiter of Augsburg; and Willy Messerschmitt as Hitler arrived at the works. After the Bf 109 demonstration, Messerschmitt took Hitler aside to show him the mock-up of a four-engined bomber – which nobody at the RLM had heard of – Projekt Nr P.1064, later to become the Me 261.

Top: Willy Messerschmitt with Flugkapitän Dr Hermann Wurster, who on 11 November, 1937 established an absolute world speed record for landplanes of 610.950 km/hr, in Bf 109 V13, D-IPKY.

Above: Eighteen months later, on 26 April, 1939, Flugkapitän Fritz Wendel (seen here with Messerschmitt) established the absolute speed record in D-INJR, the Bf 209 V-1 that was officially designated Me 109R, with a confirmed speed of 755.138km/hr.

'In 1932 I tried to design an aircraft to be as fast as possible: a two-seat light aircraft, but with an engine of only 150 hp and a landing speed of only 65 km/h (the M29). Through a carefully studied shape and smoothing of the external surfaces, the use of slotted wings and, for the first time, a single-legged undercarriage, it reached a horizontal speed of 260 km/h. Through this aircraft I learned very much that, later, I could use in the development of fighter aircraft. Therefore I have plenty of reasons to remember fondly the Europaflights.'
Messerschmitt during his speech to the Deutsche Akademie der Luftfahrtforschung (German Academy for Aviation Research), 26 November, 1937.

'With extremely limited means I designed and built a series of sports and transport aircraft which, through their high performance, served as first steps towards a high performance fighter. Soon after, when I received the assignment to develop a fighter, it was evident to me that it would have to derive from aircraft like the M23 and M29. I then tried to equip an aircraft as small and light as possible with a powerful engine, in order to create a fighter that could out-perform anything then known. This was proved clearly at the International Flying Meeting in Zürich in 1937. Since that time this aircraft (the Bf 109) has been developed constantly at a hectic pace to meet the new challenges, and improved upon over and over again, so that to this day our enemies consider it the most sucessful fighter in the world. In English circles now and then one hears the assertion that they have brought out an aircraft superior to the Me 109. Nothing can better disprove this than the list of our victories. From the steadily improving performance of the Me 109 in the course of this war, and its lasting superiority, you can see that we are actively maintaining this superiority into the future as well.'
Messerschmitt in a German broadcast, 8 December, 1942.

'As an illustration of the struggle for the right shape I would like to mention that in 1934, when the Me 109 originated, the prevalent view in (German) military circles was that the biplane was the right formula for a fighter aircraft. It was not easy for me to devlop a monoplane fighter. I had first to fight for my ideas before I could transform them into reality. Only comparative flights by the fast monoplane convinced the doubters of its superiority in aerial combat. The same conclusion had been reached in every other country and the triumph of the monoplane could no longer be delayed. What was valid for fighter aircraft was also valid for all other aircraft, including airliners.'
Messerschmitt, Lisbon, November 1961.

And a footnote from another voice:
'I have been told that a Bf 109 cost approximately 150,000 Reichsmarks in 1939, though later it became somewhat more expensive. Assuming that the Reichsmark was worth double the value of the present Deutschmark, then the most modern fighter which existed then would be worth DM 300,000 today. I look wistfully upon these figures from the past. Today the price of the least expensive jet aircraft is DM 2.5 million, and can even reach DM 6 million.'
Dr Franz Josef Strauss, then the West German Defence minister speaking about the Bf 109 in 1958.

Above left: 'In 1932 I tried to design an aircraft as fast as possible . . . through this aircraft I learned much that I could later use in the development of fighter aircraft . . . ' The racing M-29 on finals displays its slender lines, with design features later inherited by the Bf 109 – slim fuselage, high tailplane, and stalky undercarriage. Strangely, it also resembled strongly the initial Spitfire design . . .

Top: GUNNER'S VIEW. A Bf 109E-4 breaks away after a simulated attack on a Junkers Ju 87.

Above: 'Father' of the Bf 109, the Bf 108 'Taifun' flew in hundreds all over the world. Here, at the July 1937 Zurich meeting, Ernst Udet is about to give General der Flieger Erhard Milch and a woman companion a ride in Udet's personal Bf 108, D-IBVQ./*Photopress*

First Blood

Late in 1936 three Bf 109 prototypes were sent for operational evaluation to Spain, where civil war had begun in July. These were: V3, *WN 760*, D-IOQY; V4, *WN 878*, D-IALY; and V5, *WN 879*, D-IIGO*. On 9 December, 1936, Oberstleutnant Wolfram von Richthofen ordered Lt Hannes Trautloft, who had arrived in Spain on 7 August, to go to Seville airfield, there to test-fly Bf 109 V3, which had just been prepared. Unable to take off from Vitoria airfield because of fog, Trautloft had to make the journey in an ancient car and arrived next day at Seville, only to be told that the day before a young *Leutnant* had crashed V3 while attempting to take off. Trautloft, therefore, had to wait until the ground staff had prepared V4. In his diary he noted:

'*12 December, 1936*. The new Bf 109 simply looks fabulous. Alongside it the good old He 51 looks like a withered maiden, and yet only with a heavy heart can I part from her, grown grey in honour.
13 December. We are still not in warpaint. I have removed the top hat we painted on our machines until now and had a green heart painted on the aircraft instead. Thuringia, my home country and the green heart of Germany, should be here too. [Trautloft later became *Kommodore* of his Jagdgeschwader 54 "*Grünherz*', or green heart".]
14 December. At last the 109 is ready. However, there is no instructor or expert to check me out. A mechanic from Junkers [the Bf 109 then had a Junkers Jumo engine] can only explain the instruments, levers, undercarriage retraction controls and so on to me. When I ask him how V3 was "pranged" he answers laconically that "apparently the machine has a tendency to swerve to the left on take-off. "The take-off certainly is unusual, but as soon as I am in the air I feel at home in the new bird. Its flight characteristics are fantastic. When I am airborne I find an Italian Fiat fighter above the airfield. So far the Fiat has been reckoned the fastest of all Franco's fighters, but I get behind it and have overtaken it in a moment, leaving it far behind.
23 December, 1936. I have been in Seville for nearly two weeks now, as the Bf 109 goes down with one teething trouble after another. They are all trifling. First the tail wheel does not work, then the water pump, then the carburettor, then the undercarriage locking mechanism. But the repairs take time and the wasted hours mount up.
2 January, 1937. Today I have yet another emergency landing. The main problem is the continued heat, which makes trouble with the cooling of the engine and carburettor adjustment.

14 January. The Bf 109 is ready for ferrying to the Madrid front. To fly the 109 is really a joy. When I had to land at Caceres because the weather worsened, the people on the ground seemed like the strangely slow-moving inhabitants of a far-away planet. I need time to get used to the earth again. Spanish mechanics jostle each other around my 109 and marvel at this new high-speed bird.'
Hannes Trautloft ended World War 2 as an *Oberst*, with 57 confirmed victories.

In April 1937, 2.J/88, one of the four *Staffeln* of Jagdgruppe 88, the Legion Condor's fighter complement, replaced its Heinkel He 51s with the first Bf 109Bs to arrive in Spain; by that time the three prototypes had been field-tested for seven weeks. Günther Lützow, one of Jagdgruppe 88's pilots who was to gain five victories in Spain and end in World War 2 with a tally of 108 victories, described his Spanish missions of July 1937 in the 1940 edition of the Luftwaffe Yearbook:
'The enemy had broken through near Brunete, endangering the important supply route Talavera – Madrid, the loss of which would have been catastrophic. One rainy night in early July I received an urgent order that same night and be ready for action at dawn in Avila, west of Madrid. That meant covering 350 km of country roads what a prospect! At once I got everyone out of bed and had the officers and NCOs report to me. "Everything has to be evacuated", I told them, "trucks have to be loaded and a locomotive has to be found. The advance party must be ready to leave in half an hour at the latest, and the fuel truck must leave at once. We will take off at daybreak; by that time the train has to be in Avila." With only the light of pocket torches and headlamps the tents were taken down, spare parts packed and trucks loaded. My interpreter scooted off to the nearest railway station, roused the station-master out of his bed and mobilised a locomotive. The *Spiess* (senior NCO) was everywhere spurring the men on; he was both indestructible and indispensable.
'When I took off at first light I was not at all sure that everything would work out right. The Spaniards should have been able to help us out, but it was doubtful if they would have everything we needed to hand. But when we landed at Avila, the commander of the advance party was there to report to me. Thank God, this party at least had arrived! But where was the fuel truck, the most important item of all? Was it lying somewhere along the road with a broken axle? Had the engine broken down? Nobody knew. And the

*Bf 109 V5, WN 879, was indeed D-IIGO, and not as sometimes claimed D-IEKS.

27

Above: Bf 109B-2 of J/88, Legion Condor, in Spain. The first Bf 109s were hurriedly sent to Spain when it became apparent that the Heinkel He 51 biplanes were no match for the Russian, Polikarpov-designed I-15s coming into use by the Spanish Republicans. The 'Franco' markings, black cross on a white background on the tail, and colours reversed on the wings, are evident here.

Right: Two views of the Bf 109B-2 of Hauptmann Gotthardt Handrick who was 'Staffelkapitan' of 2.J/88 in Spain. Winner of the Pentathlon at the Berlin Olympic Games in 1936, Handrick appropriately marked his personal aircraft with the five Olympic rings symbol, on the propeller spinner. Note engine starting crank handle in position in latter view./ *G Handrick*

convoy with the spare parts? I was getting damnably nervous. We still had not received any orders, either, and the radio station could tell me nothing. So there was nothing to do but wait, which is most uncomfortable in such a situation.

'As if all this were not enough, the commander of Avila arrived, and since for the moment I was the ranking officer of the party, I had to report to him. He asked me if the Jus [Junkers Ju 52/3m's] could be put into action. What a question! The only thing we knew for sure was that there was AA artillery around Brunete in huge quantities. Through binoculars we had followed a mission flown by the Italians during the morning. The *flocks* [anti-aircraft bursts] that had been thrown up for a quarter of an hour on end made it look very unwise to use the good old Jus in daytime. Emphatically I advised against it. The commander listened quietly to me, but he didn't seem to understand. Well, he'll learn soon enough.

'When I got back to my *Staffel* I found that in the meantime the convoy with our living quarters had arrived. The mechanics were already working on their machines, and shortly afterwards the fuel truck also appeared. Everything was OK now. We were ready.

'Alongside us were some reconnaissance aircraft and at the other side of the airfield were the Italians with 45 Fiats – *molto bene*! Everywhere the usual protective trenches had been dug, bomb-proof rooms built and alarm systems constructed. It amused us: why all the precautions? The enemy would surely not venture across the lines. After all, there were fighters on the airfield and AA artillery too. That should be enough! But for the first time we were quite wrong.

'The enemy played all his trumps at once. They attacked, crossing the front lines singly or in groups – yes, they even daringly attacked our airfield. We had to fly standing patrols, and be ready at all times, from 0415 till 2130 hrs. We shot down some, but time and time again fresh aircraft attacked. And we had other missions to fly too. Three or four times every day we had to accompany bombers or reconnaissance aircraft, always at 6-7,000 metres. Every time we were in contact with the enemy; and every time we met AA fire on a scale we had never before experienced. We had a very difficult time. Everybody had to give his utmost, always fighting and always confronting some new experience. There was no time for reflection: we traded experiences, then they were translated into orders and used in practice. For the rest, we just flew or slept!

'To open the assault from our side, we sent bombers or reconnaissance aircraft across the front at great height to draw the enemy AA and attack it with bombs. We accompanied these aircraft across and hung about between Brunete and Madrid to attack all aircraft that

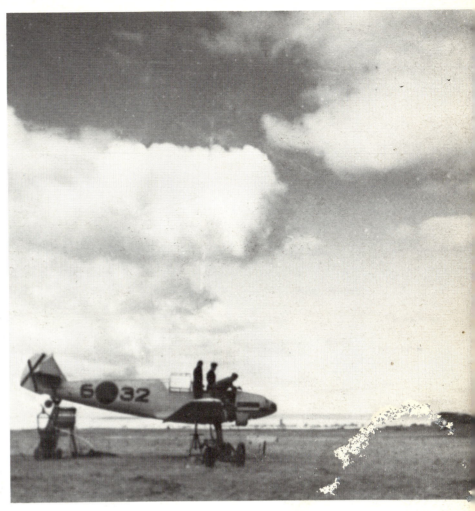

came from the fighter airfields on the other side of the capital. Ten minutes later the Heinkel He 51s would make low-level attacks against enemy 3.7cm and 2cm batteries and keep the gunners' heads down with machine-gun fire and fragmentation bombs. Then the Jus appeared, accompanied by Fiats. When we saw them would hold our breath. Flying v close to each other in a compact mass, awfully low, they looked such a ripe target for the AA. But nothing disastrous happened. The Jus droned on unconcerned and dropped their bombs on the positions in the narrow passes where thousands of reservists were lying up, wreaking havoc.

'Why was the AA so ineffective? It had no option as time and time again well-aimed bombs crashed down to destroy guns, injure gun crews and force other batteries to change position. Nevertheless some guns – and no small number at that – did obstinately fire at the black mass of bombers and scored hits, but in relation to the number of guns down below the results were minimal. Thus the plan of the Commander and his chief of staff effectively eliminated most of the AA during the crucial attack.

'Some 3,000metres above the Jus about 60 fighters were swarming. A few Fiats had

Above left: 'Rottenflieger.' Bf 109B-2 of 2.J/88 formating on his 'No 1' over the Mediterranean coastline near Benicarlo, 1938./ *E Neumann*

Left: Another view of the same Bf 109B-2. Note exhaust 'trap door' at rear of radiator./*G Handrick*

Above: HARMONISATION. A Bf 109B-2 of the Legion Condor trestled into flying position for its guns to be harmonised by the 'Fluzeugrüstpersonal' – the squadron armourers./ *G Handrick*

Right: BEAT-UP. Nine Bf 109B-2s in a mass low-level 'strafe' of their own airfield in Spain, 1938. /*G Handrick*

Below: The Bf 109's first serious enemy – the Polikarpov I-16, named 'Chato' by the Republicans, and 'Rata' by the Nationalists. To avoid capture by Franco's troops, during the Catalonian advance, three of these agile fighters fled from Figueras airfield to France, where they belly-landed at Illats on 6 February, 1939. In the period August 1936 to November 1938, units of the Legion Condor destroyed 277 opposing aircraft in aerial combat; a good proportion of which were credited to the Bf 109 pilots. It was invaluable operational 'training' for the Luftwaffe prior to the European war in the following year.

come along, but mostly it was 'Ratas' and Curtisses *versus* my small formation. Seven against 40! There was no time to aim carefully. It was turn, attack, aim at the red circle, press the buttons, pull out, gain some height, turn back, get the next one in front of one's guns, hold it – this time too many are behind me – dive down and break away for a moment to get one's breath back. Now some of them were trying to get at the Jus, smelling an easy prey. I attacked them out of the sun and pulled up – but too fiercely: the plane wallowed for a bit and lost speed. Just then a glance below found a 'Rata' climbing up at me, four small flames flickering from his engine. Closer and closer he came to me, but I couldn't do anything for the moment. I was defenceless – this was the end, I thought. But at last I got up some speed again and evaded him for a moment. Then I saw two or three behind a Messerschmitt – a comrade needed help. As fast as possible I went at them, blazing away. On and on it went, seconds became an eternity, but at last the Jus were gone and the mission has been accomplished. But there was no time to be tired. It was back to the airfield, take aboard fuel and ammo, then the same thing all over again!'

On 24 April, 1945, Oberst Günther Lützow, victor in 108 combats, was reported missing near Donauwörth, flying a Messerschmitt Me 262 jet fighter of JV 44.

A gold medal winner at the Berlin Olympic Games, 1936, was Gotthard Handrick, an *Oberleutnant* in the Luftwaffe. He was victor in the pentathlon, which consisted of horse riding, fencing, pistol shooting, swimming and running. Later he became Kommodore of Jagdgeschwader 26, and ended World War 2 as Kommandeur of the 8th Jagddivision in Vienna, credited with a total of 10 victories. Before the war he served with the Legion Condor in Spain and when the civil war ended he wrote in the *Buch der Spanienflieger* – the book of those who flew in Spain:

'In the course of an aerial combat I got to grips with a Curtiss and, as this was one of my first air fights, I was naturally convinced that I would shoot down the enemy in no time. How wrong I was! Apart from the fact that my guns did not seem to function properly, I was none too clever in my handling of the aircraft. I attacked the Curtiss from behind and he turned back, but instead of pulling up before pressing the attack, I let go immediately. In each attack I only succeeded in firing ten rounds. The Curtiss, though much slower than my machine, was very manoeuvrable and an excellent climber; moreover, he shot extremely well. Gradually we got farther and farther from the coast, and finally were five kilometres out at sea, in the vicinity of Gijon, 50-60km away from the front. It was high time to end the combat. I got closer and closer to the Curtiss, until

eventually a terrible noise told me I had rammed him. The wing of my machine was hit close to the fuselage and the controls were jammed. I went into three or four involuntary rolls, one after the other, until at last I regained control and could fly more or less straight ahead. Ought I to jump over the sea? No, thank you! The water was too cold in October. So I flew towards the land, not daring to think what I would do should someone jump me.

'At last I came in sight of the front. At Llanes airfield I could crash the machine in peace and quiet on the airfield. But then I recalled the words of the *Gruppenkommandeur*: "Where on earth are you going to find a replacement if you destroy an aircraft? Every bridge in the hinterland has been blown up and it could be weeks before you get a new machine." So I flew my unhappy aircraft on to Santander. Thank heaven, I was only 150 metres up. Cautiously I lowered the undercarriage. Whereupon a piece of the enemy Curtiss dropped off, a souvenir from one of my first aerial combats that I still keep, and now and then look at thinking that a man needs luck! After the landing I found that the right wing was done for, the fuselage full of bruises and damaged at the back, and that the tailplane needed replacement. But I was happy I had held out, because two days later the damage had been more or less repaired and she was flying again.'

Lieber Besuch
aus U.S.A.

Foreign Pilots

Left: Three of the six Bf 109s that created a great impression at the 1937 Zürich-Dubendorf meeting; from nearest, V-8, D-IPLU; V-7, D-IJHA; and V-10, in military camouflage. The other three were V-9; V-13, D-IPKY; and Udet's all-red V-15, D-ISLU.

Bottom left: 'A dear visitor from the USA' – Ernst Udet's cartoon view of 'Lucky Lindy' climbing into a Bf 109.

In all probability the first non-German pilot to fly a Bf 109 was Maggiore (Major) Aldo Remondino of the Regia Aeronautica. He was the *Comandante* of the *Squadriglia acrobatica* that performed so graciously with their Fiat CR 32s at the Zürich International Flying Meeting, 23 July to 1 August, 1937. The personal friendship between General Valle, commander of the Italian Air Force, and General der Flieger Erhard Milch made it possible to arrange – in the utmost secrecy – for Major Remondino to fly one of the six Bf 109 prototypes which had caused something of a sensation when they participated in various events at the meeting. After an introductory flight in one of the Bf 108s also on hand, the Italian was able to try out the Bf 109 just after sunrise, when Dübendorf airfield was still deserted.

Thirty-eight years later, having in the meantime become a *Generale di Squadra Aerea* and vice-President of the Italian airline Alitalia, Remondino still remembered that flight. 'The flight lasted one hour' he wrote, and I could form a clear opinion of the features of the monoplane. It was undoubtedly more advanced as far as speed and climb were concerned than our Fiat CR 32, but had remarkably inferior manoeuvrability.'

The Luftwaffe was then highly secretive about its latest fighter. Little could Milch suspect that, hardly six months after the Italians's flight, the first 'potential enemy' pilot would have already thoroughly tested a Bf 109B. A machine used by the Legion Condor in Spain had fallen into the hands of the Republicans and the Spanish Government offered the French Government an

opportunity to test the little fighter, together with a Heinkel He 111 that had been captured intact. Three French specialists arrived in Barcelona on 31 January, 1938 and were taken to the nearby airfield at Sabadell, where the two captured aircraft stood waiting.

To Capitaine Rozanoff of the French Testing Centre at Bretigny fell the task of testing the Messerschmitt, which took 10 hours' flying time. In order to make the tests as accurate as possible the air speed indicator (ASI) was calibrated by flying a measured stretch along the ruler-straight road between Tarragona and Reus. The French delegation was much impressed by the aircraft's performance and their findings were incorporated in an extensive report – which fell into German hands when France was over-run two years later in June 1940! The report stressed the negative influence exerted by the engine's torque when making a climbing turn to the right. General d'Harcourt, commander of French fighter units, was quick to signal this characteristic to his pilots when France declared war on Germany in September 1939.

The first American pilot to fly a Bf 109 was Major Al Williams, USMC, the noted US Naval flier who won the 1923 Pulitzer Trophy, and at one period held the world speed record of 266mph. Williams, a friend of General-major Ernst Udet, was touring Europe in his extremely colourful NR 1050 'Gulfhawk', a modified Grumman G22, which he used in the promotion of Gulf products. He made a private deal with Udet. The German could fly Williams' brilliant orange-painted biplane if Williams could fly a Bf 109. The temptation

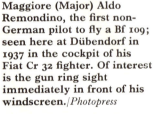

Maggiore (Major) Aldo Remondino, the first non-German pilot to fly a Bf 109; seen here at Dübendorf in 1937 in the cockpit of his Fiat Cr 32 fighter. Of interest is the gun ring sight immediately in front of his windscreen./*Photopress*

was too great for Udet, and the Luftwaffe wanted to impress the world with its new fighter.

The day was 15 July, 1938. With Udet, Williams flew to the Fieseler works at Kassel, where the Bf 109D was being licence-built. Later Williams reported:

'After inspecting the local plant, we came upon the Me 109 that was waiting for me. This was my first chance really to study the gadgets and instruments in its cockpit. Each was christened with a name that ranged anywhere from an inch to an inch and a half in length. None of them meant anything to me, and I was compelled to identify their location and their uses by following the instructions of the patient chap who explained them to me . . .

'I stalled around a little bit, until I became somewhat familiarised with gadgets and controls, retractable landing gear, controllable-pitch propeller switch, auxiliary hand pumps, manually controlled flaps, and the various gauges and main and reserve gasoline cut-off valves. Standing still, the controls were light and delicate to the touch. The engine sounded like a dream, no rattling or vibrating as in the case of aircooled radials. This was a 12-cylinder in-line job, and it ran like a watch.

'Fixing my parachute in place and snugging down for the ride ahead, I taxied out into the field. There's never a moment when the pilot of a new ship is not keenly alert for the chance of learning something about that ship's performance. Many times it's only a hint, but many times, indeed, that hint is all-sufficient to keep him out of trouble. The ground con-

trol was excellent. Without using the wheel brakes, on the way out to the take-off position, I found that a propeller blast on the rudder brought a surprisingly pleasant reaction, in spite of the fact that the vertical fin and the rudder were both rather small. The take-off was normal, and I estimated that the ground run was fully one-half the distance used by the Hawker Hurricane and about one-fourth the distance used by the Supermarine Spitfire.

'I have my own little formula to be followed in flying a new ship, and I stick to it religiously. Leaving the landing gear extended, I climbed up to about a thousand feet, set the propeller blades at the required high pitch, checked the engine instruments, and then slowed the engine down. The air speed indicator, of course, was calibrated in kilometres. I slowed the ship down to about 130 kilometres, pulled the nose up, and let it fall away. Repeating the motion again by pulling the nose of the ship up this time beyond the stalling angle, I watched it sink evenly and steadily, with no hint of crankiness.

'Flying along at about 20 miles above stalling speed, the ailerons had excellent control along with a fully effective rudder and elevator. This was all I could ask. A few turns to the right and to the left at reduced speed, a couple of side slips, and I was ready to come in for my first landing. It has always been my practice, irrespective of the new type of ship I'm flying, to take off, go through such procedures to become adjusted to its flight characteristics, and then go around for the first landing within two minutes after the take-off. This is to make sure of at least one

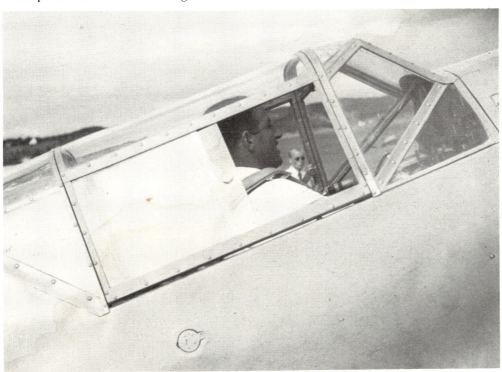

Dipl Ing Carl Francke, a Rechlin test pilot, in his Bf 109 at Dübendorf. He won the Climb and Dive contest of this meeting.

Udet's friend, Al Williams, standing on the left float of his personally-financed Kirkham-Williams would-be entrant for the 1927 Schneider Trophy race. Had he won, the USA would have gained permanent possession of the trophy; but Williams' aircraft was not ready in time.

routine approach for a landing while the engine is still good.

'I was amazed when I brought the Messerschmitt around, tipped it over on one side, and slid toward the ground. Leveling out we got away with a three-point landing with the air-speed indicator reading about 105 kilometres per hour. The Me 109 was an easy ship to fly, and with one landing behind me, we went to work – or rather to play.

'For the first take-off, I had set the flaps at about 15 degrees to facilitate the take-off. On the way in for a landing I found that 20 degrees on the flaps was a more suitable angle of attack. The controls, sensitive ailerons, and tail group were fully effective to the time the wheels touched the ground. So much for that. This, after all, was supposed to be an outstanding single-seater fighter, and in the half hour allowed me, I was determined to find out if the Messerschmitt was or was not what it was cracked up to be.

'The supercharger boost gauge was calibrated in atmospheres instead of inches of mercury. I recall a little difficulty in remembering what my instructor had told me about the permissible supercharge boost at low altitudes. I said this Messerschmitt was fast. The Germans had said so, too, to the tune of 350 to 360 mph, and their claims were demonstrated to be accurate. It is also interesting to note, in 1940, that the British concede the Messerschmitts to be good for 354 mph.

'The most delightful features of the Messerschmitt were, first, in spite of its remarkably sensitive reaction to the controls, the ship showed no disposition to wander or "yaw" as we call it; neither was there any tendency to "hunt". It was a ship where the touch of a pianist would be right in keeping with the fineness of the response. And, likewise, I am sure that any ham-handed pilot who handled the controls in brutal fashion would soon be made to feel ashamed of himself. Seldom do we find a single-seater that does not stiffen up on the controls as the ship is pushed to and beyond its top speed. I checked the control reaction in three stages – one as I have already mentioned, slightly above the stalling speed, and the controls worked beautifully.

'In the second stage, about cruising speed, a movement of the control stick brought just exactly the reaction to be expected. And at high speed, wide open, the control sensitivity checked most satisfactorily.

'Then I wanted one more check and that was at the bottom of the dive where the speed would be in excess of that ship's straightaway performance. So down we went about 2,000 feet with the air speed indicator amusing itself by adding a lot of big numbers – to a little over 400 mph. A gentle draw back on the control effected recovery from the dive; then up the other side of the hill. It was at that point that I subjected the ailerons to a critical test. I had pulled out of the dive around 400 mph and had started in a left-hand climbing turn. The ship was banked to about 40 degrees with the left wing low. I touched the right rudder, pressed forward on it slowly but steadily, moving the control stick to the right, and that Messerschmitt actually snapped out of the left-hand climbing turn into a right-handed climbing turn. That satisfied me. From there on, I tried every aerobatic maneuver I had ever executed in any other single-seater fighter with the exception of the outside loop and the inverted loop.

'The guns on this ship – five of them, all hunched on the fuselage – certainly made me feel as if I were aiming guns and not flying an airplane. In addition, I was particularly intrigued to find the control stick equipped with a tiny flap which was hinged to lie on top of the stick when not in use and to be swung forward and down – parallel with the front edge of the control stick handle. This little flap was the electric trigger which completed the circuit, when pressed by the forefinger, to operate all five machine guns. I found this trigger sensitive to the touch and extremely light, later ascertaining that a pressure of 3 milligrams was required to close the circuit and actuate the guns.

'The trigger arrangement was the final little detail which brought me the impression that instead of actually flying an airplane upon which guns were mounted, I was actually aiming a delicately balanced rifle.

'When you see a man take off in a type of airplane he hasn't flown before, you can tell before that chap returns to the ground whether he likes the ship or not. If the ship is tricky and cranky or he is not satisfied with it, he'll probably make some big figure eights and maybe a few little dives, or a couple of loops. But if he really flies the ship and rides the sky with it, amusing himself with all sorts of aerobatic maneuvers, you can walk up to that chap as soon as he completes his landing and tell him you are glad he liked the ship. And that is exactly what Ernst Udet said to me after I had zoomed the field a half dozen times and overstayed my specified time in the air. As I taxied into the line, Udet, keen as a whip, and never missing a trick, walked toward me saying, "Al, you like that ship huh?"

'The longer one is at the flying business, the more firmly convinced he becomes that he knows very little about it. I must say, however, the Messerschmitt Me 109 is the finest airplane I have ever flown. It was a very happy day for me thus to enjoy the opportunity of flying and studying one of Germany's first-line single-seater fighters. I was told, of course, that the performance of the Heinkel 112 was about the same as the Messerschmitt, and I have been assured on this point, repeatedly. As far as I know, I'm the only pilot outside the members of the air force who has ever flown a first-line Messerschmitt Me 109.

'Along with its delightful flight characteristics, the visibility in this Messerschmitt is all that a fighter pilot could reasonably ask. There are a great many single-seater fighters in the world that I have not flown, but I had formed my opinion of the flight characteristics of the Messerschmitt after studying it on the ground and before flying it. And those estimates were confirmed in flight. I had made my own estimates of the performance and maneuverability characteristics of a lot of other single-seater fighters, and I'd be willing to wager that none of them represent the general, all-around flight and fighting characteristics possessed by the Me 109.

'There was only one critical question I had about the Messerschmitt that I flew, and that concerned the retractable landing gear. The wheels were hinged to fold outwards, toward the wing tips, retracted. This placed additional weight in the wings several feet from the fuselage.

'I asked Udet about this and he informed me that this would be changed. According to the new plan, the wheels would fold inward, toward the center of the wing, and in retracted position would be neatly tucked directly under the fuselage, a desirable feature in regard to balance and maneuverability. However, photographs I saw at a much later date did not show the change, but I still think this would be a definite improvement. Before dismissing my flight in the Me 109, it is necessary to include a comment on that already offered concerning the accessibility of the engine for maintenance service. I will give it to you point blank and let you estimate its value. The engine of the Messerschmitt can be removed, replaced with another – ready to go – inside of 12 minutes.

'You can imagine the uproar of doubt and incredulity in official circles when I returned to the States and spread that word around. The reason for the uproar was quite obvious, in that in very many instances, between 24 and 36 hours were required to remove one engine and replace it with another in many of our standard types of fighting planes. But, when other Americans returned home from an inspection of the German Air Force and told the same story, great impetus was given to the development of a quick motor replacement in service ships. . . . The Germans had developed the technique and trained the ground crews to effect this change of engines in the specified length of time on the open airdrome – given, of course, decent weather conditions.

'It was explained to me that, from a tactical standpoint, this ultra-rapid change of motors was of utmost importance. For instance, a pilot returning from an active front to his own airdrome could radio ahead and notify the field force that ne needed a new engine. By the time he landed, they could be ready for him.

'Ordinary service to an aircraft, such as filling the gasoline tank, checking and replenishing the oil supply, and reloading ammunition belts, requires between ten and fifteen minutes. The new development, therefore, enables the Germans to change an engine while the rest of the service is going on. It's startling performance – namely, yanking one engine and replacing it with another, and turning it over to the pilot inside of 12 minutes'.

The next American to pilot the Bf 109 was

Trans-Atlantic hero Charles Lindbergh visits the Augsburg works. From left: Lindbergh, Willy Messerschmitt, Fritz Wendel, Lilly Stromeyer (Messerschmitt's future wife), Herman Wurster, and Willy Stör.

no less a personality than Charles Lindbergh, the internationally famed trans-Atlantic solo flier. On Wednesday, 19 October, 1938, Lindbergh was flown from Staaken, Berlin to Augsburg in a Junkers Ju 52/3m. In his diary he noted: 'After inspecting the factory we walked to the flying field, where demonstration flights of the 109 and 110 were made for us. The speed and manoeuvrability of the 109 was, of course, most impressive. A small plane always looks much faster than a larger one and is quicker in manoeuvres. On the other hand it was amazing to see a two-engine plane (the 110) do acrobatic flying almost as well as the smaller type. After watching the demonstrations I made two flights in the

Messerschmitt 108, a small, four-place, all-metal, low-wing monoplane with slots, flaps, and retracting gear. Both the 109 and 110 have slots and flaps. It was originally planned that I fly a 109, but the Germans did not want Détroyat [a French military pilot] to fly this plane, and did not want to let me fly it without asking him to do so. They had no objection to him flying the 108. Consequently, I will fly the 109 at Rechlin after this trip. Détroyat told us – including the Germans with us – that some of these French pilots had tested a captured 109 in Spain. It had a 211 Junkers engine and made 465 km/h. Everyone laughed. This incident is well known to both French and German aviators. The French were apparently much impressed with the characteristics of the 109.'

Two days later, 21 October, Lindbergh finally had the opportunity to fly a Bf 109 at the Luftwaffe Test Centre at Rechlin (E'Stelle Rechlin). Laconically he noted down: 'We next inspected the Messerschmitt 110, then passed on to the 109 I was to fly. I got in the cockpit while one of the officers described the instruments and controls. The greatest complication lay in the necessity of adjusting the propeller pitch for take-off, cruising, and diving. Then there were the controls for the flaps, the retracting gear, for flying above 2,000 metres, for locking and unlocking the tail wheel, and for the other usual devices on a modern pursuit plane. After studying the cockpit I got out and put on a parachute, while a mechanic started the engine. Then, after taxying slowly down to the starting point, I took off.

'The plane handled beautifully. I spent a quarter of an hour familiarising myself with the instruments and controls, then spent 15 minutes more doing manoeuvres of various types – rolls, dives, Immelmanns, etc. After half an hour I landed, took off again, circled the field, and landed a second time. Then I taxied back to the line. The 109 takes off and lands as easily as it flies.'

What the Americans probably did not know was that an American pilot had already shot down a Bf 109, and on the same day another American pilot had been shot down by one. In Spain, Frank G Tinker, flying a 'Rata' in a squadron manned mainly by Russians, and operating from Manzanares de la Sierra, shot down the Bf 109 flown by Höness on 13 July, 1937; while Harold 'Whitey' Dahl, flying a 'Chato', also in a unit manned mainly by Russian pilots that operated from Campo Soto, was brought down by a Bf 109 and taken prisoner. For their 'services' the American pilots were paid more than handsomely, earning some 18,000 pesetas per month. The ordinary Spanish workman then averaged 120 pesetas monthly.

Hermann Wurster briefing Lindbergh in a Bf 108 four-seater, prior to Lindbergh's first flight in a Bf 109.

First 'Tommy'

Above: The first Luftwaffe pilot to shoot down an RAF aircraft in WW2. Feldwebel Alfred Held joined Infantry Regiment 20 in April 1932, started gliding and then joined the Luftwaffe. Serving first with JG Richthofen, he next joined JG Horst Wessel. He also served in Spain with the Legion Condor, and was severely injured in a crash on 30 June, 1938.

Top right: Vickers Wellington bombers of 149 Squadron RAF, from Mildenhall, pictured at Le Bourget aerodrome, Paris on 10 July, 1939 in their pre-war codings. Less than two months later some were wrecks in the Jade Bight . . .

Bottom right: The 'Gneisenau', probably the target for the Wellington shot down by Held, seen here mounting an Arado Ar 196 of 10. (See)/ LG 2, based at Travemünde. Like many other German warships, the 'Gneisenau' replaced its Heinkel He 60s with Arado Ar 196's of Bordfliegerstaffeln 1./196 and 5./196, based at Wilhelmshaven and Kiel-Holtenau, only a few weeks before war came in 1939.

One hour after the war between England and Germany started, at 1200hrs on 3 September, 1939, Flying Officer Andrew McPherson of 139 Squadron RAF took off from RAF Wyton in a Blenheim IV, N6215. His orders were to reconnoitre the German Fleet bases. At 1650hrs he landed back at Wyton with the news that, notwithstanding the misty weather, he and his crew had observed a number of warships in the Schillig Roads, off Wilhelmshaven. Next morning McPherson was again over Wilhelmshaven and Brunsbüttel, and as a direct result of his findings the first RAF bombing raid of the war was ordered. Here was an opportunity to deal a heavy blow to the enemy Kriegsmarine; the battleship *Admiral Scheer* was riding at anchor in the Schillig Roads, together with an armada of cruisers and destroyers, while the *Scharnhorst* and *Gneisenau* battlecruisers were moored in the Elbe off Brunsbüttel.

The ships were attacked by five Blenheims of 107 Squadron from Wattisham, of which four failed to return, and five Blenheims of 110 Squadron, also from Wattisham, of which one was lost. The attack, executed with great courage and determination, failed completely in its objective, due mainly to the old-pattern bombs used, all of which either missed the targets or failed to explode on impact. A further force comprising five Blenheims of 139 Squadron, six Hampdens of 49 Squadron and six Hampdens from 83 Squadron – both latter units based at Scampton – failed to find any targets because of the weather. Later in the day, 4 September, after the weather had improved slightly, six Wellingtons from 9 Squadron (Honington) and eight more from 149 Squadron (Mildenhall) attempted to attack the *Scharnhorst* and *Gneisenau* off Brunsbüttel. One of the 9 Squadron bombers was to become the first RAF aircraft to be shot down in WW2 by a Luftwaffe pilot.

Long before the Wellingtons approached their targets the German fighters had been alerted, and Bf 109Es of II./JG 77 lay waiting at Nordholz airfield, 12km south of Cuxhaven, and only 45km north-east of Wilhelmshaven. This *Gruppe* had its origin in the Fliegerstaffel (J) Kiel-Holtenau which had been inaugurated on 1 October, 1934. In 1937 it was retitled I.(1) JG 136; in 1938, II./JG 333; and finally in May 1939 it became II./JG77. Its commander was Oberstleutnant Schumacher, who held this appointment until succeeded by Major Harry von Bülow-Bothkamp at the end of 1939. One of the unit's pilots, Feldwebel Alfred Held (*Held* means 'hero' in German, incidentally) was responsible for the Luftwaffe's first victory over the RAF. The 26-years old pilot, who hailed from Weissenburg, near Nürnberg, reported his victory to the *PK-Kompanies* (similar to war correspondents) in the following terms:

'We were alerted around six in the afternoon. In the shortest time possible we were off towards the enemy. Now at last things were getting started! Our formation soon reached Wilhelmshaven but nothing was to be seen over the harbour. So we turned away to the Jade Bight, where we could hear AA guns booming even above the noise of our engines. But while we were turning away I spotted three unidentified aircraft, with AA shells exploding among and behind them. We raced towards them, gratefully noticing that the AA guns were holding their fire. But the enemy aircraft had disappeared. They had been engaged by the AA guns of a German warship that we were then flying over and when I glanced down I could see two English aircraft lying in the water – twin-engined bombers, one of them still burning. So the first Tommies had met their fate.

'But while we were circling above this memorable spot I suddenly observed, very far away, another twin-engined aircraft which I recognised as English. Our formation curved towards it. The *Leutnant* leading our formation positioned himself above the Tommy in order to attack, but unfortunately he was still too far away to shoot at him with any chance of success. I was much nearer to the Englishman and did not hesitate to engage him.

'With my *Staffel* comrades still relatively far behind me, I already had the Englishman in my sights. Calmly and confidently I fired the first bullets into his aircraft, feeling as hardened to combat as if I had already shot

down a dozen Englishmen. However, the bomber's rear gunner wasn't going to allow me any complacence. As I streaked he fired one burst after another at me. Despite fiercely concentrating all my senses on the job, I managed to make out clearly every single detail of the Wellington bomber, even its various crew members. Whether that rear gunner was a good shot and had hit me I could not see for the moment. So, unperturbed, every time I had a free field of fire I shot at the enemy aircraft. Was I a better shot than the Englishman? Time and again we rushed past each other, machine guns hammering away and engines howling like maddened beasts, and thus twisting about we strayed far out over the Jade Bight.

'As if the Englishman sensed the death-blow coming he dived his bomber to get more speed and escape from my fire. Lower and lower I forced the Tommy, but still he defended himself desperately. Then – I could hardly believe my eyes – a long flame shot from the left side of the bomber. Was this the finale? Already the aircraft seemed to be out of control and wallowing about. A last burst of fire from my guns – and that

was enough. The aircraft dropped its nose and fell. I throttled down and circled to follow the Englishman's descent, but already there was just a burning pile in the water, and that lasted only a few seconds. Then the waves closed the grave and foaming wavetops glided above it as before.

'My first victory! I realised this as I was flying home and was extremely happy. When I proudly landed my fighter after rocking my wings, my comrades ran wildly towards me from all sides. They knew about my victory already and all wanted to shake hands heartily with me. I had trouble fending off their congratulations and eager questioning. 'The Victor of the Jade', I heard one of them cry. But first I had to examine my aircraft, which brought me back safely. How lucky I had been! The Tommy had only hit me once.'

A short time later Feldwebel Troitsch of the same *Gruppe* shot down a second bomber. He reported to the PK-men:

'We were flying above the German Bight off the Elbe estuary. I noticed the Englishmen far below us, very low over the water. As my comrades had apparently not yet spotted the enemy formation, I told them. I was flying in the front of our formation so I was the first to fire. When we got nearer I recognised the Englishmen as Wellington bombers, twin-engined aircraft with a rear gunner at the end of their fuselages.

'Two of the aircraft immediately turned towards the low-hanging clouds and disappeared. The third one was right in front of my guns and I closed to 100 metres to be sure of hitting him. At 50 metres the Englishman's left wing broke off and a flame shot from the fuselage. Shortly before the Englishman had returned my fire, though without hitting my machine, I found out later. By the time the bomber was engulfed in flames I was only 20 metres behind him. The burning tail fell off and streaked past, just above my machine, so that I had to dive to avoid being swallowed by the flames. I dived away to the right and followed the bomber, which dropped from some 400 metres into the water, where it quickly disappeared, leaving just an oil slick. I then attacked a second bomber which appeared among the ragged clouds. At full revs I raced after him and again his rear gunner tried to rake me, but this Tommy had no success either. Unfortunately I lost the Englishman, as we were soon into cloud. But as I curved away I found myself fired on by the Englishman's front gunner. I dived immediately to follow the bomber, but then realised we were too far out to sea.'

This day's operations, with its disastrous results for the RAF, was described thus in the *Adler von Friesland*, Luftflotte 2's own newspaper:

Left: Though practice with a 12-bore against clay pigeons (as here at the RAF's Central Gunnery School) was valuable training, the Wellingtons' air gunners were severely hampered by fixed, ie, non-revolving, gun turrets during the combats over the Jade Bight, giving Held and his comrades a relatively easy task.

Right: Alfred Held on 9 October, 1939, just over three weeks before his death in an air collision on 2 November. His decorations include the Silver Spanish Cross (on right pocket); Iron Cross, 2nd Class, awarded for his victory on September 4; Badge of the Spanish Military Order of Merit, 1st Class; and the Spanien Feldzugmedaille (Spanish campaign medal).

Below: When war started in September 1939, all Bf 109Bs had been replaced by Bf 109Ds and Es in the various fighter units. Here, a Bf 109B-1 and its pilot, Keil, pose at Döberitz in 1938./
W Schäfer

'The attack against German naval bases along the North Sea by some 20 English longe-range bombers of the newest type was a total failure. The bombs dropped caused no damage. Fighters and AA artillery brought down, with certainty, 10 English aircraft in the area of the Coastal Commander, East Frisia alone. Four of them were brought down by a man-of-war of the Kriegsmarine.'

The corresponding entry in the Operational Record Book (Form 540) of 9 Squadron RAF was terse:

'Nos 2 and 3 of A Flight did not return to base and were reported missing. First squadron to draw blood.'

Feldwebel Alfred Held received the Iron Cross, Second Class for his first victory. It was also to be his last. One month later his elder brother, Wachtmeister Friedrich Held died on the Western Front. On 2 November, 1939 Alfred Held's aircraft was accidentally rammed by another German aircraft and he crashed to his death.

At the time Held's 'first' victory was widely proclaimed in the German Press. In April 1963, however, Generalmajor a. D. Carl Schumacher, who in 1939 had been Kommandeur of II./JG 77 said that he had always believed that Feldwebel Troitsch was actually the first to shoot down an RAF aircraft.

Erster Luftsieg

Left: 'Jagdflieger'. Major Helmuth Wick, commander of JG Richthofen, in his Bf 109E-3, autumn 1940, checking instruments prior to an 'Einsatz' (war sortie). By this time Wick was the most successful Luftwaffe fighter pilot, apart from Werner Mölders and Adolf Galland./*Bundesarchiv*

Below: The 'Pik As' (Ace of Spades) insigne of JG 53 being spray-stencilled onto Leutnant Wick's Bf 109E.

Helmut Wick was born in Mannheim on 5 August, 1919. On the outbreak of war he was serving as a fighter pilot with JG 53, which left its base at Wiesbaden-Erbenheim for airfields behind the Siegfried Line and was entrusted with guarding the German border in the Eiffel mountains and Saarbrücken region. On 22 November, 1939, as a *Leutnant* with I./JG 53 flying a Bf 109E, Wick obtained his first victory (*erster Luftsieg*) when near Phalsbourg he shot down a French Curtiss H75A, No 95 of GC II/4, from Xaffévillers. Wick later became commander of JG2, 'Richthofen', and wrote a series of articles for *Der Adler*, entitled *Hetzjagd am Himmel* (Drag-hunt in the sky). This was how he described his first victory:

'It was in November 1939. We were stationed at an airfield behind the Siegfried Line and kept ourselves busy with a very necessary, if not exactly stimulating task; border-surveillance flights. Whenever an old fighter pilot hears those words he backs away; nobody wants to know about border-surveillance, which offers nothing but hour-long boring flights without contact with the enemy. It was 22 November when I first saw the roundels of an enemy aircraft. As the French did not fly over the German border, for once, we decided to get nearer and visit them at home. The wind from the east quickly took us towards France. Suddenly I saw a whole gaggle of aircraft flying at some 6,000metres near Nancy, and realised at once that they were not German. We started flying in a circle, but immediately two aircraft separated from the gaggle and hurtled down at us.

'Now I recognised them – Curtisses. We dived to get away (I was flying with just my *Rottenkamerad*) and as we anticipated, the two unsuspecting Frenchmen dived after us. When I started a climbing turn one of the Frenchmen was sitting right behind me. I can still remember perfectly how I could see his roundels when I looked behind. It was one of the most memorable moments of my life and I confess that seeing those red-white-blue roundels was rather exciting – all the more so because the Frenchman was firing away with all his guns. Realising that somebody is behind you, shooting at you, is very unpleasant; after all, it was my first aerial combat. However, I remembered the lesson given to me by Mölders, my instructor – 'In a critical situation, first get away, then watch for developments.'. I pushed the nose of my bird down and, being much faster than the Frenchman, shook him loose rapidly. When I could no longer see him I thought that the others must be above me to my left. But nothing was to be seen there. Could they be to the right? When I looked in that direction I could hardly believe my eyes. I was looking straight at four radial engines sprouting small red flames. As usual in such cases, a ridiculous thought crossed my mind: are they allowed to shoot at me like that? Just as quickly I was deliberating; shall I try to get away again? No! Now I'll get at them. One *has* to go down. I clenched my teeth and pushed stick and rudder to the right.

'When I completed my turn the first one already shot past. The second followed right behind him and I attacked this one frontally. Looking right into his guns firing was nasty. We were too near each other to get any results. He jumped over me, and now the third one was there, as near as the second. I shifted my machine to get him nicely lined up and aimed just as I had learned at school.

Left: Luftwaffe fighters along the French border in the early days of the war only occasionally met the French 'Ballons de protection' . . .

Below: . . . More frequent were encounters with Curtiss 75s of the French Armee de l'Air, which, after some initial successes, proved to be no match for the Bf 109E.

Right: Another 'opponent' was the French 75-mm anti-aircraft (AA) gun. These existed in several versions but basically dated from WW1-vintage designs, and were sorely inadequate for their purpose by 1939.

Far right: Backing the AA defences, the French used location and listening devices such as this cumbersome machine.

At my first shots I saw some metal pieces coming off the Frenchman; then both his wings gave way. Closely behind him came the fourth Curtiss, also firing at me, as I could see by the fire from his gun barrels. I was not hit, however; everything just passed me by. The first two climbed again, but I did likewise so that they could not catch me. It was now time for me to go home as I was getting low on fuel. My *Rottenkamerad*, whom I later found safe and sound at base, had lost me during the diving and twisting.

'On the way back I did not meet any more Frenchmen – though I wasn't sorry about that! The first aerial victory of my life was enough for one day. But after I had shaken off the other Frenchmen and was flying alone towards Germany at high altitude, I suddenly got the 'hunting fever' and relived the various phases of the tense combat that I had fought against four times superior forces. My first aerial victory! Never have I sat more happily in my faithful bird than on that unforgettable 22 November.

'I was so confident of being victorious in any future combat – and I hoped it would be soon – and so engrossed in my happiness, that I lost my way. I simply flew in a general easterly direction and was soon completely

lost. This was not too serious: as soon as any large recognition feature showed up I could get orientated again. Very soon I saw far below the autobahn winding through the landscape. I was back over Germany already and when, soon after, a wide river that could only be the Rhine showed up, followed by an airfield, nothing could go wrong – even if it wasn't my home field. I landed with the last drop of my fuel. It was Mannheim. I think I gave the good refuelling people a raspberry because they did not work fast enough for my liking, but I was in a hurry to get home again and waggle my wings. On the very short trip to my base airfield I was happy as a schoolboy that I too could fly over our command post waggling my wings. And I did it thoroughly. My mechanics were over the moon too. I realised how excited I was when I kept trying to get out of my cockpit without noticing that my seat harness was still fastened.

'The most remarkable thing about my first victory was that I had wanted to turn back on the outward flight. My machine had been washed down shortly before take-off, and at altitude ice had formed, which was annoying. For some time I vacillated between a desire to turn back and remove the ice, and the hope that something might turn up. This hope triumphed over the wish to return, and even today I'm happy about that.'

On 28 November, 1940, almost exactly a year later, Wick was himself shot down south of the Isle of Wight and parachuted into the English Channel. He was never found. In that year he had become one of the Luftwaffe's most successful fighter pilots, with a credited score of 56 victories. His conqueror was Flight Lieutenant John C Dundas, DFC, flying a Spitfire of 609 Squadron RAF. Wick was Dundas's 13th victim but seconds later Dundas was himself killed by Wick's *Rottenkamerad*.

Far left: LUFTSIEGE. 21 victory symbols on the rudder of Wick's Bf 109, with Wick (3rd from left) receiving the congratulations of his pilots. His 20th 'Luftsiege' (victory) brought him his Ritterkreuz (Knight's Cross to the Iron Cross) award. Of interest are the Luftwaffe kapok-filled lifejackets being worn by Wick and several of the pilots, plus the signal flare cartridges strapped around the thighs of the two pilots at right of photo.

Far left, below: As one of the Luftwaffe's most successful fighter pilots in the summer of 1940, Helmuth Wick was promoted to command the elite JG 2 Richthofen. He is seen here shortly after, being interviewed by official war correspondents from the German Rundfunk (Radio).

Left: The Old and New – Hermann Göring, commander of the Richthofen Geschwader in 1918, congratulates Helmuth Wick in 1940. Between them is General Hans Jeschonnek, then Chief of Staff of the Luftwaffe, who committed suicide in August 1943. Note the Geschwader Richthofen band on Göring's greatcoat sleeve.

Below: '. . . He was seen to parachute into the Channel but has been missing since . . .' – 28 November, 1940.

Battle over England

Bf 109Es operated against England from British soil! After Germany seized the Channel Islands in 1940, some Bf 109s were based there during the Battle of Britain. Here a Bf 109E-4 of JG 53 'Pik As' is being refuelled at La Villiaze airfield, Guernsey with the aid of a locally commandeered lorry (J H Miller went out of business several years ago). On 9 August, 1940, a Bf 109E-1 of I./JG 53 collided with a flak-tower on Guernsey, killing the gun crew.

'While we are climbing our engines drone away evenly. To my left and right fly the other machines of my *Staffel*. The morning mists above the French west coast slowly recede behind us. The altimeter indicates 4,000 metres . . . 5,000 metres. We put on our oxygen; we go for altitude. Direction – London. Our mission is *Freie Jagd* (Free Hunt). We cross the Channel. From our height it looks like a broad river. Small clouds cover the white coast of Old England. We are on 'the other side.' The clouds that form a layer over southern England at an altitude of between 2,000 and 3,000 metres become denser and denser. Every opening is watched closely. It is through these that 'the others' will come at us. A *Deckungsrotte* (two fighters working together) watch the sky above and behind to counter any surprises from those directions. Visibility is perfect – one can clearly make out Canterbury. Soon the flak will start; this area is already well known to us for that.

This Bf 109E-4 carried the
personal emblem of
Helmuth Wick, in front of
the air intake, and an
unusual form of
Balkenkreuz on its fuselage./
E Obermaier

'Suddenly something crackles in our head-sets. 'Achtung! Six to eight aircraft below us in the cloud gap.' One hears this often and usually they are our own aircraft on their way back, but this time we know for sure that they are not ours. In addition their line-formation is suspect. So beware! They climb higher. The dark silhouettes of Spitfires stand out clearly against the white cloud cover. I reckon they are 1,000 metres below us. But dammit, why doesn't our *Staffel-führer* attack now? When they spot us our chance will be gone. We continue flying a sharp left turn but our leader, an old hand, knows why. And suddenly I understand. Of course, the attack has to come from out of the sun.

The uncertain moment before any combat has now gone – now we can start. I am flying the third machine behind our *Staffelführer*. We attack while diving and rapidly get nearer. A smoke trail curves downwards, falls into the clouds – our leader has got the first one. The next Spitfire now looms large in front of me. Its cockades shine provokingly. Flip the safety catch – push the buttons – dammit! He has spotted me and turns steeply away. At the same moment I have another in front of me, flying in the same direction. I am near enough to ram him, so clear are the sharp

Top left: Adolf Galland rose rapidly to fame as a fighter pilot and leader during 1940. Here he is wearing an immaculate white flying overall, and a strictly non-issue polka-dot neck scarf./ *A Weise*

Bottom left: Adolf Galland's aircraft when commander of III./JG 26 in the later stages of the Battle of Britain, at Caffiers, France. On the rudder are 22 Luftsiege symbols – by the end of the war there were to be 104./*A Weise*

Top and above: Two views of Feldwebel Beese's 'Yellow 11' of 9./JG 26 – a Bf 109E-3 – after a crash-landing in the coastal dunes near Calais, August 1940. The bullet which ripped into the aircraft from behind, indicated, was stopped by the pilot's armoured head-rest./ *A Weise (both)*

wing-tips, the cooler, the cockades. Guns and cannon hammer away and the Spitfire explodes in a ball of fire. I watch the Tommy go down trailing black smoke. He is the fourth of his tribe to get acquainted with the guns of my loyal '5'.

'What is that – smoke trail very close to my machine? All is tension again. But suddenly they are gone. I can just see a Tommy upside down behind me disappearing downwards, burning. Bits and pieces trail behind him. A 109 passes me, flying faster, than I and I recognise a comrade of my *Staffel*. So it was he who shot down the Tommy behind my back.

'In a few seconds everything is over. A quick glance at my instruments – everything is still all right . . .'

This account by Leutnant Erwin Leykauf of JG 54 was written after a combat on 11 November, 1940. He ended the war as an Oberleutnant, credited with 33 victories.

Top left: 'Schwarze' 4 – Black 4. A Bf 109 belonging to 8./JG 54, based at Le Mans, March 1941./*A Weise*

Centre left: WAITING. A scene to be found on practically any fighter station of the Luftwaffe – and the RAF – during the hot summer of 1940. Members of 7./JG 54 at Soesterberg, July 1940; from left, Feldwebel Michel; Leutnants Behrens and E Leykauf. Note the Staffelwagen just behind the pilots' row of deckchairs./*E Leykauf*

Below left: Pilots of 9./JG 2 Richthofen at Octeville, Le Havre in 1940, discussing the next mission. From left: Uffz Neumann (killed October 1940); Staffelkapitän Oberleutnant Röders (killed Spring 1941); Uffz Rudi Rothenfelder; Feldwebel Maier (later killed in action); Oberfeldwebel Brunkhorst, nicknamed 'Ghandi'; and Gefreiter Schaaf (later killed in action)./*R Rothenfelder*

Bottom left: Bf 109Es of 8./JG 54 at dispersal on Guines airfield, France, (near Calais), 1940. Schwarze Drei (Black Three) was flown by Leutnant E. Leykauf./*E Leykauf*

Bottom right: During the French campaign the idea of using the Bf 109 as a 'Jagdbomber' – 'Jabo' (fighter-bomber) had already been considered – to the dismay of the fighter pilots. Illustrated is one such 'Jabo', Bf 109E-4/B of II (Schlacht) /LG 2 at Calais-Marck in October 1940. The SC 250 bomb is chalk-inscribed 'Hals und Beinbruch' (literally, 'Neck and Leg Break' – a traditional 'Good Luck' greeting by German airmen prior to any mission, dating from WW1) – and signed 'Uncle Hugo'./*A Weise*

WREN ODDENTIFICATION

When Willy produced his one-seater,
And began building castles in Spain,
They believed he had got a World-beater,
Till it met Sydney Camm's Hurricane.

Willy's gone and made another,
Something like its elder brother—
Wing-tips rounded, spinner's bigger.

Unbraced tailplane ends its figure.
One-O-nine F is its name—
F for futile, not for fame.

Above: World-famous were the brilliant Wren 'Oddentification' series of aircraft recognition cartoons published during the war by the artist, E A 'Chris' Wren – an original approach to the serious subject of teaching aircraft recognition. This is how Wren 'saw' the Bf 109E and Bf 109F versions./ *Chris Wren*

Below: In the same vein were the cartoon series 'Salient Characteristics' by Cummings, which appeared in the official British publication 'Aircraft Recognition'. This panel illustrated the principal recognition features of the Bf 109G in the journal issued April 1944./*Crown copyright*

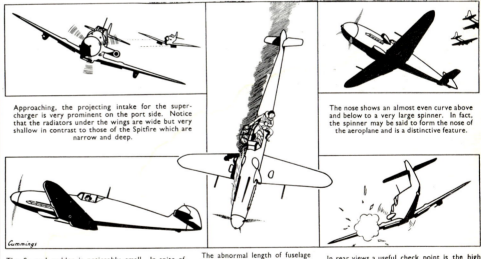

Approaching, the projecting intake for the supercharger is very prominent on the port side. Notice that the radiators under the wings are wide but very shallow in contrast to those of the Spitfire which are narrow and deep.

The nose shows an almost even curve above and below to a very large spinner. In fact, the spinner may be said to form the nose of the aeroplane and is a distinctive feature.

The fin and rudder is noticeably small. In spite of its straight leading-edge the general appearance is rounded and there is a characteristic "heel" to the rudder.

The abnormal length of fuselage from wing to tailplane becomes visible in any plan view. Notable are the almost pointed wing tips and the small size of the tailplane.

In rear views a useful check point is the high mounting of the tailplane. In this view the fuselage, because of the inverted-Vee engine, has the appearance of squatting close on the wing.

Fighting the Spitfire

ERWIN LEYKAUF

Hauptmann Friedrich Geisshardt, 'Kommandeur' of III./JG 25, seated in the cockpit of Spitfire VB RF-E (AA 940) in 1943. The Spitfire that belonged to No 303 (Polish) Squadron landed undamaged in France. Geisshardt was shot down shortly after this photograph was taken while attacking 8th US Air Force bombers attacking the Erla VII Repair Depot near Antwerp on 4 April, 1943,
A. Weise

During what was later called the 'Battle of Britain', we flew the Messerschmitt Bf109E. The essential difference from the Spitfire Mark I flown at that time by the RAF was that the Spitfire was less manoeuvrable in the rolling plane. With its shorter wings (2 metres less wingspan) and its square-tipped wings, the Bf 109 was more manoeuvrable and slightly faster. (It is of interest that the English later on clipped the wings of the Spitfire.) The Bf 109s also had leading edge slots. When the 109 was flown, advertently or inadvertently, too slow, the slots shot forward out of the wing, sometimes with a loud bang which could be heard above the noise of the engine. Many times the slots coming out frightenened young pilots when they flew the Bf 109 for the first time in aerial combat. One often flew near the stalling speed in combat, not only when flying straight and level but especially when turning and climbing. Sometimes the slots would suddenly fly out with a bang as if one had been hit, especially when one had throttled back

to bank steeply. Indeed many fresh young pilots thought they were pulling very tight turns even when the slots were still closed against the wing. For us, the more experienced pilots, real manoeuvring only started when the slots were out. For this reason it is possible to find pilots from that period (1940) who will tell you that the Spitfire turned better than the Bf 109. That is not true. I myself had many dogfights with Spitfires and I could always out-turn them.

One had to enter the turn correctly, then open up the engine. It was a matter of feel. When one noticed the speed becoming critical – the aircraft vibrated – one had to ease up a bit, then pull back again, so that in plan the best turn would have looked like an egg or a horizontal ellipse rather than a circle. In this way one could out-turn the Spitfire – and I shot down six of them doing it. This advantage to the Bf 109 soon changed when improved Spitfires were delivered.

When, many years later, I got to see the Spitfire 'Pilots' Notes' it became clear to me why on many occasions we were able to surprise Spitfire pilots – at least in the beginning. Many times we wondered how it was possible. Today it seems to me that simply flying the Spitfire was a full time job judging by the contents of the 'Pilot's Notes'. The Bf 109 was much simpler, technically speaking. For example we had the *Propellorautomatik*, automatic propellor pitch setting. When one gunned the engine, the pitch was automatically reduced. But we could also alter the pitch setting by hand, and this could be used to get a higher rate of fire from our nose guns which were synchronised with the propellor. Flying level and wanting a higher rate of fire, like for instance when attacking a bomber, one had only to set the pitch setting at 11 o'clock (12 o'clock being the maximum). This very low pitch resulted in a very high rpm and thus a high rate of fire.

Late in 1940 or early in 1941 I had an interesting encounter with a Spitfire, a combat 'in reverse' in effect. I was flying at 4000 metres (13,000 feet) above Maidstone, a noted fighter airfield, on my way home. We had been in a dogfight, our formation had been scattered and I was alone. Many times after an aerial combat we were short of fuel and the red lamp frequently came on when we were halfway across the Channel. This time the red lamp flickered on and off while I was still over England.

By radio I tried to find out if any of the others were in the vicinity. 'Igel Fünf' confirmed that he was. I called, 'This is Igel Einz, come nearer', and gave him my position south of Maidstone.

I asked 'Hanni?' (altitude)

'Hanni four thousand.'

'Good, my Hanni is also four thousand, come nearer'. I looked around but didn't see anything, wondering where he was. At last I spotted him, coming up from behind getting nearer and nearer until I called.

'Mensch, tuck in close, my red lamp is already flickering'.

He answered 'Viktor, Viktor, I'm coming'.

At last he came closer and I started looking at my map. I reflected that even if my engine was to stop, I still could get across the Channel. (From 4000 metres above Dover one could just reach the French coast in a glide and we were over the coast near Dover.)

I called, 'Stay to my left'.

'Viktor, Viktor'.

Then I looked behind me and thought what a strange aircraft it was! I couldn't see the two radiators below the wings but quickly noticed the red spinner (which, incidentally, none of us had – contrary to what has been claimed later). I had never seen a Bf 109 with a red spinner – and suddenly it dawned on me – it was a Spitfire!

He was already perhaps only two or three hundred metres, flying very fast and eventually he came alongside. I could only think that his guns had jammed. I was so frightened that I opened up the throttle and there we were, suddenly flying in formation! And now something funny happened. I thought: '*Donnerwetter*, if I keep on flying like this I'll get in front of him and he'll have me cold. To make it worse I am low on fuel!

Probably he was thinking at that same moment: 'Dammit, when I dive away, he'll get behind me and that will be my lot!'

'What do *we* do now?'

At that moment I saw him throttle back. So I said to myself 'there is only one thing to do, to throttle back', so I throttled back.

And there we were flying very slowly in formation with me thinking: 'If I stall and fall away I will have him on my tail but if he stalls then I am behind *him*!'

I watched him hanging there, very near, perhaps two wingspans away, and it made a formidable impression upon me. Probably he was also thinking that if he were to make a wrong move he would be lost. I knew, too, that there was little hope for me as I had very little fuel left; but this was something he didn't know!

There was nothing else he could do but keep on flying as slowly as possible.

Then he opened his canopy. I can still see him today. He wore a leather flying helmet and had pushed his goggles up. Then I thought about flaps and I lowered them. I looked at him and saw that he had also his flaps down. The seemingly huge roundels on his fuselage dazzled me. Now we were at minimum flying speed, neither wanting to advance on the other. But then he could no longer hold on. He had to open his throttle... I could see black smoke coming from his exhaust stubs. He advanced a bit and I thought: 'Now I'll get you'. I kept on flying as slowly as possible but he receded again and once more we were flying alongside. Then... with our left hands we waved to each other... a unique occurrence!

For quite some time we kept on flying side by side, always in the direction of France. The unspoken question for us both was: How do we lose each other? There was only one possibility: to get away as suddenly as possible'. Then all at once, I could no longer see him and I thought 'Now he has got you after all'. I pushed the stick forward but then saw his blue belly, falling away far below me; he disappeared.

We had by now arrived halfway across the Channel and he had probably had to turn back because his fuel was getting low. Of course he was not to know that by coincidence my own fuel warning light was on.

Oberleutnant Erwin Leykauf, photographed in Russia in 1943.

Above Tundra, Ice and Steppe

Above: SNOW DISPERSAL. A Bf 109F of III./JG 53, 'Pik As' being prepared for a mission during the bitter cold of the 1941-42 winter campaign./*W Schäfer*

Right: The first Luftwaffe pilot to shoot down a Russian aircraft after the start of the war with Russia. Oberleutnant Robert Olejnik with his 'Wart' (mechanic) Uffz Mackert, standing by the tail of Olejnik's Bf 109F-2 (Wk Nr 6743), and the rudder victory tally of 21 'Luftsiege'./*R Olejnik*

The first German pilot to shoot down a Russian aircraft in World War 2 was Robert Olejnik, now living in retirement in Oberschleissheim where, before the war, he was an instructor at the Fighter Pilot's School. He recalls:

'From the middle of February 1941 I was *Staffelkapitän* of 4./JG3, as an *Oberleutnant*. On 1 June we moved from St Pol airfield in northern France to Breslau-Gandau, by way of Strasbourg and Regensburg. All members of the *Geschwader* had to be on duty from dawn to dusk; letters were censored and all leave cancelled. We were totally in the dark about our future activities or eventual missions. On 19 June the complete II./JG3 left with all its Bf 109F-2s for the airstrip at Dub, some 8km from the Polish town of Zamosc, which lay 80km south-east of Lublin, and about 50km from the nearest Russian soil. On the occasion of the Midsummer Night celebrations we lit a huge bonfire and had the usual cold drinks. Then around midnight there came a telephone call from the *Geschwader*: 'All unit commanders immediately to the command post'. There each received an envelope with a mission order, but it was only to be opened when the code word 'Barbarossa' was given .It was impossible to think about sleep; though we all lay down in our tents to rest, we were excited and full of tension. On 22 June, 1941, at about 0230hrs, the password came through. I opened my envelope and found that an attack against the Soviet Union was about to begin.

'Everybody in the *Geschwader* knew that I was an early riser and that I liked to fly the first missions at dawn, so I made the first take-off. About 0330 hours I took off with my *Rottenflieger* to reconnoitre Russian airfields near the border, watching for enemy fighters. In doing so I discovered that on every enemy airfield two or three Russian fighters were stood at the ready. After flying over several airfields, and on the way back, I again flew over the first airfield I'd seen. As I got nearer I saw that two aircraft were already manned by pilots. At a height of 7-800metres I flew a wide turn round the airfield and watched closely. After one and a half circuits, I saw the Russians start their engines and taxi out, then take off immediately. As they were obviously looking for a fight, I attacked the first 'Rata' with a height advantage of 3-400metres, and succeeded in shooting it down with only a few rounds in my first attack. Comparing times with my *Rottenflieger* later, this happened at 0358hrs on 22 June, 1941. The second fighter was probably shocked by seeing one of his unit going down burning and flew away, because I could no longer find him. Returning over our own airfield, I waggled my wings three times. Unbelieving, my comrades shook their heads – most of them had only just woken and were peering sleepily from their tents.'

Olejnik had already obtained eight victories in the West and later rose to *Major*. In November 1943 he went to Erprobungs-Kommando 16, which took a part in developing the Messerschmitt Me163 rocket fighter, where he suffered a severe accident.

Murmansk was the gateway through which much of the war material being sent by England and America entered the Soviet Union. Month after month the German and Finnish armies tried to capture this vital harbour, or at least to interrupt the rail link to Leningrad, more than 1,000km to the south. They never succeeded. On various airfields west of Murmansk, mostly on Finnish territory, were stationed the Bf109s of Jagdgeschwader 5, 'Eismeer Jäger' (Hunters of the Arctic Sea). This unit, which had been organised in January 1942 from sections of I./JG77 and IV./JG1, constantly operated over the lonely, endless tundra in very bitter weather conditions. In the spring of 1943 some war correspondents visited 6./JG5 to gather first-hand stories for 'those back home'. *Staffelkapitän* from June 1942 was Oberleutnant Heinrich Ehrler who, at the time of the following interview, was credited with 77 aerial victories and the destruction of 11 locomotives. On Saturday, 27 March, 1943 he shot down five Russian aircraft in one mission:

'We had taken off with six machines (109Fs) to do some 'free hunting' and went to look for the enemy over his own airfields. This time we were lucky and bounced a gaggle of Airacobras, Kittyhawks and IL.2 attack aircraft west of Schonguij, about 20km south of Murmansk. Altogether there were some 30 aircraft, which had apparently just taken off, intending a surprise raid on one of our bases. The surprise was to be for the Russians, however. The enemy formation flew on a westerly heading, very low over the tundra – first a close formation of 15 aircraft, with the rest following in pairs. Four of us attacked the main formation. Such an attack always moves fast. That day it lasted hardly four minutes before I had sent down numbers one to five. Two hit the ground east of Tuloma, the third on the west bank. I got the fourth and fifth in a wide right turn. The next candidate was now flying to my left, slightly in front of me, and I was at a height of only 150metres. Below me to the left three Kittyhawks and an Airacobra were twisting around.

At the moment I was about to open fire at the enemy flying in front of me, there was a

loud bang in the cockpit and I was immediately surrounded by heavy smoke. What had happened? A heavy machine gun bullet had hit right behind the engine in my ammunition feed and exploded one of my own cannon shells. After I had dived away I tried to ascertain the extent of the damage. The engine was still running perfectly. But I had been hit in the left leg and hand by some very small splinters, a very large hole had appeared in my left wing, and the tip of the right wing had been blown off. The wounds hardly hurt, but after several minutes of debating whether I should resume fighting or fly home, I decided, reluctantly, to go back. It turned out later that I had been hit twice and the machine was only held together by a very thin metal strip. Another fight and it would surely have given way.'

Eventually, facing a courtmartial following the sinking of the *Tirpitz*, and then holding the rank of *Major*, Heinrich Ehrler was killed on 4 April, 1945 while flying with the *Geschwaderschwarm* of JG7. It was just a few weeks before the war ended.

The next day, 28 March, 1943, also saw some heavy fighting in the air. Leutnant Theo Weissenberger, one of 6./JG5's most successful pilots and, before the war, a former glider pilot and NSFK *Sturmführer*, explained how he obtained his 69th, 70th and 71st victories:

Top: GREEN-HEART. Bf 109G-5/R3 of II./JG 54 'Grünherz' returning from a sortie over the Eastern front. Clearly visible is the 'Beule' – hump – covering the breeches and ammunition magazine of the Rheinmetall-Borsig MG 131 guns. Note too the fuel drop-tank's minimal clearance with the ground – an added hazard to take-off and landing for Bf 109 pilots./*Bundesarchiv*

Above: Pilots of Jagdgruppe z b V. Petsamo – later, in May 1942, incorporated in JG 5, 'Eismeer' – on arrival at Kirkenes airfield in Norway on 1 June, 1941. This photo was taken at 2330 hours, by the light of the 'midnight sun' . . ./ *M Villing*

Above: Bf 109G-4s of II./JG 3.
While based at airfields in
the Wiesbaden-Mannheim
area for a rest period, the
whole 'Geschwader' was
titled 'Udet' in late 1941,
after Ernst Udet's suicide./
Bundesarchiv

Right: Line-up of Bf
109G-4s of II./JG 3. Aircraft
nearest camera was flown
by the 'Gruppe' adjutant;
while the third machine was
that of the 'Geschwader'
adjutant. Note speckled
camouflage applied to the
engine sections, contrasting
with the remaining overall
markings./*Bundesarchiv*

64

'We had taken off to protect some fast bombers and met about 20 Kittyhawks and Airacobras. Within two minutes I shot down two Airacobras, and three minutes later a Kittyhawk, my 71st victory. Then I got mixed up with a lone Kittyhawk but simply could not get him in front of my guns during the twisting combat that followed. It was a real merry-go-round. At last, after what seemed an eternity, I got behind him so that I could fire a burst at him. The Curtiss flew right through it, turned upside down without catching fire, and crashed vertically. I saw it hit the ground beside a lake and explode.'

Weissenberger eventually chalked up a total of 208 victories and survived the war. On 10 June, 1950, he died in a racing car accident at the Nürburgring.

Feldwebel Hans Döbrich shot down two Hawker Hurricanes on 22 September, 1942, his 15th and 16th victories:

'We were on escort for a bomber formation and met about 40 Hurricanes and Curtiss Tomahawks over the enemy airfield at Murmaschi. Eight of us attacked and completely surprised the enemy formation. I saw three Russians get out of their aircraft and take to their parachutes as soon as they were shot at! Out of the two Hurricanes I shot down two black specks also jumped, sinking to the ground below their white parachutes. During this combat I counted a total of 12 who jumped by parachute; all the time one or two slowly sinking white spots could be seen. At the end we counted 12 white spots on the ground round the airfield – 12 parachutes – and 16 smoking and burning wrecks.'

Oberfeldwebel Albert Brunner, a flying instructor before joining 6./JG5, described his 39th, 40th, 41st and 42nd victories:

'We took off when the alarm sounded. Low-flying enemy aircraft were attacking a neighbouring airfield. During the approach to the airfield I shot down a Tomahawk, and then suddenly there was a gaggle of Airacobras. I engaged four of them and had soon shot down two. My fourth opponent I attacked frontally. Suddenly there were all kinds of noises in my plane; the engine stopped, pieces flew off my wings and tail. Nothing else to do but out and down. I was lucky to spot a frozen lake nearby and succeeded in performing a belly-landing on its frozen surface. After setting my machine afire, I simply waited because I knew my comrades would search and find me. Sure enough, two 109s appeared overhead and spotted my emergency landing field. Shortly after a Fieseler Storch landed right beside me – to the surprise of some mountain troops nearby. I went home.'

On 7 May, 1943, Brunner had to abandon his aircraft, but was too low for his parachute to open fully. His friends recovered his body.

Just before his death, he told another war correspondent of an eerie experience when he shot down his 14th and 15th opponents in the late summer of 1942.

'We were standing by at readiness on our airfield at Petsamo. A formation of Junkers 88s was going to attack a Russian airfield near Murmansk and we fighter pilots were to accompany them as protection. We hadn't flown for four days and our fingers were itching. The bombers took off and we followed suit. You know how things are when you are flying. Details of the earth vanish rapidly, and the land below changes from moment to moment. Here along the Arctic Sea front it is full of variation. Many reefs are to be seen, and many small islands lie like stranded wrecks in the surf. But we who had flown this route before, over and over again, hardly noticed it all. I still remember perfectly the tune I was humming: "If I were a little bird and had two wings, I would fly to you . . ."

'We had gained a high altitude and it was time to put on our oxygen masks, but I waited some time before doing so. I kept on humming my little song. Suddenly, I heard the voice of the *Staffelführer* over my radio: "Hey! Who do you think you are singing like that, Father Christmas? Have you gone nuts?" He was right: only a madman would be singing. The rebuke called me back to my senses "God"! I thought, 'have I been dreaming?" Now it was time to put on my

Above: HERALDRY. The standard outside of the 'Gefechtsstand' (Command Post) of JG 54, 'Grünherz' at Siwerskaya; displaying the individual insignia of I., II., and III Gruppen. Throughout 1942 this 'Geschwader' was constantly on the move, from one 'hot spot' to another./A Weise

Right: Deadly enemies since the Spanish civil war; a Bf 109F-2 of II./JG 54, flown by the 'Geschwader' adjutant, standing cheek by jowl with a captured Russian 'Rata' (Polikarpov I-16) on the Eastern front in the spring of 1942./Bundesarchiv

Centre right: Muscle-power is used to shove this Bf 109F-2 – the personal aircraft of the 'Gruppe' commander of II./JG 54 – into a makeshift dispersal bay./Bundesarchiv

Bottom right: 'General Winter', Germany's most implacable opponent throughout the Russian campaign, provided a daily chore for the ground crews during the winter of 1941-42. The markings on this Bf 109 indicate it was usually flown by the 'Gruppe's' Technical Officer.

oxygen mask, because we were climbing higher and higher. It became imperative to keep one's eyes open because enemy fighters were about. Hurricane and Tomahawk – the names told you where they came from – and those agile, fast-as-lightning Airacobras carrying a cannon and four machine guns. In front of us were some small clouds, coloured like mother-of-pearl. I heard the urgent voice of my *Kaczmarek*, a *Leutnant*. "Look out! Enemy above to the left!" Now I too could see three silver specks in the direction of the sea, about the same height as ourselves. They were still a long way off. Then, while I was deciding what we should do I heard in the radio – very clearly and distinctly – a female voice!

'None of us understood what was happening. This female voice out of the blue surprised us so much that at first nobody noticed that she was speaking in Russian. She sounded shrill and sharp. Nobody understood what she was saying. Still

recovering from my amazement I heard someone mutter: "Shut up, you silly bitch." Then – I don't know who it was – somebody said: "Nitschewo, Madka, nitschewo". I've never forgotten what follows. An insolent, brutal laugh, so shocking that I still hear it in my mind. Certainly it wasn't one of us, but whether it was the laughter of a woman I cannot say. Again the laughter rang out over the air. Suddenly I got mad. Any misgivings were dispelled: the hunting fever gripped me. We were just three against three – a fair fight: the three of us and the three silver specks that apparently did not want to see us. I started a turn – again I heard that hideous laughter, even more repulsive and I shot the first one down from the turn. Then I had to let the *Leutnant* have a go, because he had only recently joined us and needed his first victory. However, nobody should think an aerial combat is that easy. It takes a lot of nerve to cope with the thousand unforeseen events and imponder-

Above: 'General Mud' was the second enemy of any invader of Russia; as illustrated by this Bf 109G-2 of 4./JG 54, 'Grunherz' on its return to Siwerskaya after a sortie./*Bundesarchiv*

Right: The extreme climatic conditions on the Russian front called for unorthodox solutions to some problems of maintenance. Here a home-made wooden 'hangar' has been erected around this Bf 109F of JG 54. Note absence of swastika marking on tail./*W Schäfer*

ables; often one is astonished that things have turned out all right.

'I saw the *Leutnant* shoot down his first enemy while I covered him from the rear. I watched how neatly he got closer, saw his burst of fire, and then his opponent going down burning. But I kept wondering about that laughter. Somewhere there had to be somebody on our frequency who could actually see us, because right after the *Leutnant* shot down his man, the laughter sounded again – shrill, as if coming from Hell. 'God!. Shut up', I cried. I shot down number three – now I had my 14th and 15th victories – yet the sneering laughter peeled out again. Were they trying to frighten us?

Since hearing that laughter, the *Staffel* has scored over 500 kills. Where did the female voice come from? The answer proved to be simple. Somehow it had got on to the same frequency by chance or on purpose – who knows? We heard later that the woman had been giving a lecture – on cooking!'

Hungarian Escape

One of the many air forces to use Bf109s was the Royal Hungarian Air Force (*Magyar Kiralyi Legiero*), which first operated the type against the Russian Air Force and later against the USAAF. In the spring of 1943 the first Bf 109s were delivered to Hungary and Daniel Holeczy – then a *Leutnant* in the RHAF, but in 1975 a BAC 111 Series 500 captain with the German Bavaria airline – well remembers his first flight in a Bf109:

'At that time I considered myself an experienced pilot, with some 300hours on the Fiat CR32, Fiat CR42, and the Heja (Hungarian-built version of the Italian Reggiane Re 2000.) The controls of the 109 were not as light as those of the Italian machines. An Italian fighter moved like a pencil – you had an immediate reaction. In the 109 you had to use some force – the reaction was there but it was heavy. The German aircraft were hard, heavy, coarse, more difficult to fly, but they were much faster. The 109 had a very narrow track and during take-off and landing you had to work hard to keep it straight, as opposed to the Heja whose undercarriage was very wide and therefore easy to keep straight. Suddenly we jumped from around 800 to 1,200hp – that was a lot of horsepower in those days.'

One of the first Hungarian pilots to score a 'victory' while flying a Bf 109 was Sergeant Dezsö Szentgyörgyi, at the end of 1942. Unhappily for him his first 'victory' proved to be a Luftwaffe Heinkel He 111, which was forced to crash-land! Though there were no casualties, congratulations were hardly forthcoming. This episode did not prevent him becoming the RHAF's leading ace, with 34 victories accredited to him by the end of the war.

On 18 June, 1942 two young Hungarian fighter pilots graduated from the RHAF Academy as second Lieutenants. As Hungarian ranks are placed behind the name, these were Debrödy György hadnagy and Kenyeres Miklos hadnagy, and both were mighty proud to be then assigned to 5/2 v.szd (*vadasz szazad* – fighter squadron.) The unit operated with Heja's, soon to be replaced by Messerschmitt Bf 109Gs, and together with

5/1 v.szd, made up 5/1 v.oszt (*vadasz osztaly* – fighter group). It was better known as the 'Puma Group' from the group's insignia, a blood-red puma head, designed by the group's commander Aladar de Heppes von Belenyes alesredes (*alesredes* – wing commander), a professional soldier of noble birth. Debrödy was to end the war with 26 confirmed victories, Kenyeres with 18 and de Heppes with eight. The Puma Group's motto translated as 'Our leader is courage, luck is our wingman' – a curiously appropriate one in the context of the subsequent adventures of the two freshly-graduated fighter pilots. Debrödy recalls the story thus:

'Uman airfield at the end of January 1944. East of Uman, a Russian town about half-way between Kiev and Odessa, units of the German Wehrmacht are surrounded by the Red Army, and the Luftwaffe has undertaken to supply the pocket with food and ammunition. Junkers Ju 52/3m are to be used for the job. There are two airfields within the pocket, but as these are under enemy fire the supply aircraft are using two emergency fields. The Ju 52/3ms have to fly across 40 to 50km of enemy-held territory bristling with AA guns and intensive Russian fighter activity. Escort for the unarmed, lumbering *"Tante Ju"* is provided by 10/JG 51, whose *Staffelkapitän* is Oberleutnant Günther von Fassong, and the Hungarian 5/2.v.szd, commanded by Josef Kovacs szazados (*szazados* – captain). Because of the short range of the Bf 109s used, a second sortie is necessary when the Ju aircraft fly back carrying wounded and sick soldiers.

'On 1 February, as on most other days, I drive to the airfield early, together with Miklos Kenyeres, expecting another sortie. I already have 15 victories to my credit and the air activity holds promise of more. Heavy clouds hang very low, yet we soon receive the order for another escort mission. Quickly we contact the Jus and escort them safely to the

Above: General Magyarossy inspecting the 'Puma' Group on the Eastern Front, 1943. At left, Major A de Heppes, Group Commander; Captain Gyula Horváth; the General, talking to Lt Kalman; Lt George Pavay-Vaina; and far right, Lt Debrödy György./*G Debrödy*

Top right: Second Lieutenant Debrödy climbing out of his Bf 109G-4, Summer, 1943./ *G Debrödy*

Centre right: Two Luftwaffe officers (far left) talking with Lts S. Paszthy, G. Debrödy, L. Molnar, and Bejczy of the 'Puma' Group, 1943./ *G Debrödy*

Bottom right: An emergency landing by an Hungarian Bf 109G at Umany airfield Russia, in mid-1943./*G Debrödy*

beleaguered pocket. As we are flying back under the clouds, looking for possible strafing targets so that we will not have used all this fuel for nothing, a Yak 9 suddenly drops out of the clouds right in front of me, though just a little out of range. This unexpected gift diverts my attention so much that I completely forget to look for his comrade. (As it turned out, he came out of the clouds behind me, in front of Kenyeres.) Unfortunately our radio is not working today, so Kenyeres tries to divert the attention of the second Yak by firing at him, even though he has little chance of hitting him. Meanwhile I am busy trying to get within range and aim for a certain kill, when suddenly there is a loud crashing sound. Heat and black smoke blown in my face makes me realise that my engine is on fire and that for me the mission is over. Meanwhile Kenyeres has succeeded getting into range and shoots down the victorious Yak – Kenyeres' 18th victory. The bullets stop flying around my 109.

'I jettison my canopy, but my low altitude forces me to abandon any hope of taking to my parachute. I am over a dense forest area, but am lucky to spot a reasonably-sized

meadow within gliding distance. Ploughing up the ground poses little difficulty, but I have to admit that I am quite shaky as the result of this unexpected development. Being well drilled in emergency procedures, my first reaction is to destroy my radio equipment. Luckily uninjured, I jump from my crippled aircraft and start to run, at the same time looking at my surroundings. Some 600 to 700metres away I see khaki-clad soldiers emerging from the edge of the surrounding woods. And at the same moment – I hardly dare believe my eyes – a 109 turning sharply, lowering its landing gear and flaps, and landing almost parallel to the path taken by my own 109. Then I remember how, a few months ago, Kenyeres and I tried out the possibility of seating two in a 109, and how we had agreed that two normal-sized pilots in summer clothing, wearing no parachutes, would be able to fly a 109 if the canopy was left off. In an Olympic spurt I start running towards the other 109. As soon as it stops the canopy flies open, then off, and I recognise Kenyeres dumping his parachute and flying jacket, all the while waving and shouting at me. When I get to the 109 I have already thrown away my jacket and Kenyeres is sitting deep in the seat pan. At the same time the Russians, probably realising they have little chance of capturing me alive, start using their weapons. Above the noise of the 109's engine ticking over I can hear the whine of bullets and, I vaguely remember, explosions – possibly from mortar fire.

'I jump on Kenyeres' back, riding him piggy-back style and trying to reach the rudder pedals, as he asks me: he will operate the stick and throttle lever. My head is completely exposed over the windshield and I am gripping desperately the two handgrips in the corner of the windscreen as we attempt to take off. The first blast of the revved-up propeller blows away my goggles and flying helmet, so I cannot see a thing. Kenyeres frantically shouts for rudder control, but it doesn't help. He has to stop again. We try to sort out our handling problems, then start again. We gather speed and suddenly – I don't know how – the bumping stops and we are airborne! But though we have solved one problem, we soon have plenty of others. With the undercarriage and flaps retracted, the 109 picks up speed, and then I feel the increasing pull of the slipstream. Its suction strives to separate me from Kenyeres and the aircraft. The only holds I have are the two hand grips and my knees jammed on Kenyeres' waist. The combination of icy wind, tremendous suction and – probably – near exhaustion soon brings me to the point where I am willing to give up. In desperation I start to bite on Kenyeres flying helmet – my only possible means of communication with him. He gets the message and, not needing much visibility now anyway, crouches even lower and to one side so that I can find a little shelter behind the windscreen.

'It is pointless to wonder what would happen if a Russian fighter should drop out of the clouds now, so we both concentrate on flying the aircraft and fighting the wind and cold. Getting near to Uman, Kenyeres starts his preparations for the landing, and as the undercarriage and flaps come down, our speed is reduced and so is the slipstream and suction. The lessened strain on my hands and knees signal the approaching end of our nightmarish journey. With reduced speed we are able to exchange a few words about the landing, but I am reluctant to stick my head out again, even by an inch, to give him the minimum visibility needed for a safe landing. I do so only when he brings the speed down

Top right: COMRADES. Miklos Kenyeres (left), Kalman (centre), and György Debrödy, at Umany airfield, April 1943. Before long Kenyeres was to rescue Debrödy from certain capture behind the Russian lines; and shortly afterwards become a prisoner himself./*G Debrödy*

Centre right: Hungarian armourers servicing and re-arming the engine-mounted 20-mm Mauser MG 151/20 cannon and the 30-mm Rheinmetall-Borsig MK 108 gun./*G Debrödy*

Right: Another view of some Hungarian armourers checking over the guns of a 'Puma' Group Bf 109G. The magazines of the two 13-mm Rheinmetall-Borsig MG 131 fuselage-installed machine guns held 300 rounds for each gun./*G Debrödy*

72

and we are floating just above the ground. Down below, the ground crew recognise the markings on Kenyeres' 109 as it comes in to land, but at the same time realise that it has a strange profile. After a surprisingly good landing on Uman airfield, and once the propeller is still, we crawl out of the good old 109 with deep gratitude in our hearts. We start hugging each other and I am close to tears with emotion. Only now does the reason for the strange profile become clear to the ground crews. Needless to say, the shouting, celebration, hugging and eager questioning is endless.

'Nervous reaction works differently in different people. For the remainder of that day Kenyeres walks around, all alone, not wanting to speak about the sortie any more. In contrast, I have the urge to prove to myself that the adventure has left no mark on me, so I make another sortie in the afternoon – though, I confess, with a pounding heart.

'Two days later, on 3 February, we both get the same assignment again. The ceiling is only 200metres. On returning we run into heavy AA fire, and I see Kenyeres' 109 hit and start to burn. His body catapults from the aircraft and when his parachute opens I see an object fall away; he has lost one of his boots. I watch him landing in the trees. But he is moving as he hangs from the straps, and waves at me as if to say "So long". Circling the spot where he landed, I notice Russian soldiers already approaching. There is just nothing I can do for my friend, who so valiantly risked his life and freedom for me at almost the same spot. I circle once more and bid him goodbye with my wings. Shortly after I have to make a forced landing, wheels down, in a meadow, having run out of fuel. But I am on our side of the lines.'

Thirty two years later Kenyeres was living in Spain, and Debrödy in the USA. But they never miss a chance to visit each other and are occasionally joined by their former commander, Aladar de Heppes – the 'Old Puma'.

Top left: Scene at Veszprem airfield, summer 1944. A Bf 109G-5 of the 'Puma' Home Defence Regiment./
A de Heppes

Centre left: One of the 'Puma's' Bf 109Gs being manhandled to dispersal at Veszprem airfield, summer 1944./*A de Heppes*

Left: Aladar de Heppes von Belenyes, Group Commander of 5./1 v.oszt (Fighter Group) on 30 May, 1943, after obtaining his first two victories with his Bf 109, VO+39./*A de Heppes*

Repairing the Bf109

Top and above: Two aspects of a trial installation tested at Deurne airfield. Liquid oxygen was injected into the engine's air intake to increase its ceiling. On the first test flight of this Bf 109F on 11 March 1943, Erla VII's chief test pilot Hans Fay reached a height of 13,000 metres (41,000 feet) but had to jettison the canopy before landing as it was still completely covered with ice after descending to 1000 metres (3,000 feet).

During the Polish campaign various German manufacturers had to organise, at only eight days notice, convoys consisting of three trucks equipped as mobile workshops, complete with lathe, welding gear and the like – the *Werkstattszüge* – to repair Luftwaffe aircraft immediately behind the front lines. These were manned by specialists from various departments of each works. When the Wehrmacht swept through Belgium, Holland and France, these *Werkstattszüge* followed close on the heels of the armoured divisions. More effort was soon asked of the German aviation industry. On 8 June 1940, after Belgium's capitulation and during the last throes of French resistance, Feldmarschall Göring ordered Generalmajor Thomas to Göring's command train 'Asia' at Givet, France, near the Belgian border. Thomas was then Head of the Department for War Economy and Armament within the German forces' supreme headquarters, and was duly ordered by Göring to make a number of provisions, including the establishment of large-scale repair depots – *Reparaturbetriebe* – for German forces in the various occupied countries. Thomas lost no time and only days later several firms within Germany's aviation industry were 'invited' to set up such repair

depots, among them the Erla Maschinenwerk GmbH of Leipzig. This firm, founded on 18 July, 1934, had been licence-building Messerschmitt Bf 109s since 1937.

Ingenieur Fritz Bartsch, a long-serving staff member, was selected to organise a *Reparturbetrieb* in Belgium, where in the meantime the Department for War Economy and Armament had found a suitable location. This was the former Minerva Works at Mortsel, a suburb south of Antwerp, conveniently situated near the Deurne-Antwerp airfield and close to a railway siding. It had been the place where – until halted by bankruptcy – Minerva cars had been built, rivals in quality and price to the famed Rolls-Royce. By 20 June Bartsch was in Antwerp, but soon left for Dunkirk to acquire as necessary transport for the repair depot, five lorries abandoned by the British Expeditionary Force. As soon as he returned he hired some 50 local craftsmen and sought contact with various local contractors and suppliers who would be willing to work for the Germans. The Minerva works buildings were cleaned up, a modern office building constructed (which still stands today) and, near the end of June, the first damaged Bf 109s began to arrive by lorry. During October 1940 some Junkers 87s were also repaired as well as the Bf 109s, but this was stopped when Junkers themselves set up a repair depot at Courcelles, north of Charleroi in Belgium. In December Bartsch, now works manager, or *Betriebsleiter*, was seconded by Peter von Schalscha-Ehrenfeld, another long-serving member of the staff. Necessary tools and machinery were bought in various parts of occupied Belgium and France, many of them in Paris, and by the new year, 1941, Frontreparturbetrieb GL Erla VII was a going concern.

Trainloads of damaged Bf 109s arrived at the depot and were swiftly stripped down completely. Damaged items were either discarded or repaired and placed in storage racks alongside undamaged and overhauled

Below: Civilian Belgian workers repairing Bf 109 fins at the Erla VII repair depot at Mortsel, near Antwerp.

Bottom: Works Manager F Bartsch (dark suit, centre) conducting some German official visitors around the depot.

assemblies. Fuselages and wings were put into calibration cradles and, where necessary, re-adjusted, then stored. From the stock of stored items, completely overhauled Bf 109s were then assembled; to all intents and purposes an assembly line was eventually set up. Serviced engines were delivered from the depot operated by Daimler-Benz in adjoining buildings. Great care was taken to ensure that the latest modifications were incorporated during overhaul, including the installation of the most recent factory conversion sets – *Umrüst Bausätze* – so that some repaired Bf 109s from Erla VII were more up to date than those produced by the aircraft industry itself. As a final step, the repaired Bf 109s were carefully cleaned and polished and then taken by lorry to the nearby Deurne-Antwerp airfield, 3Km away by road and the location of Erla VII's rigging and test-flying department. At the airfield the former Stampe-Vertongen factory, where prior to the war the delightful SV.4b trainers had been built, was taken into use.

Once assembled, repaired Bf 109s were thoroughly inspected and then test-flown by Erla's works-pilots. Then, after acceptance by the RLM controllers, the aircraft were flown to assigned units by Luftwaffe pilots. One of the first pair of Bf 109s to be repaired at Erla VII, a Bf 109E-1, was test-flown on 16 July, 1940. As a finale to the test, a high-speed dive was started, but the pilot was apparently unable to pull out. The Messerschmitt dived straight into the ground, killing its pilot before the eyes of the men of II./KG3, then operating Dornier Do 17z aircraft from the airfield during the Battle of Britain. Soon between five and seven Bf 109s were being test-flown every day and, after a spell of bad weather, 50 or more could often be seen standing ready to take to the air. When it was being test-flown the aircraft bore no normal identification markings, simply the first letter of the individual pilot's name, chalked in white on the fuselage: F stood for Fay, G for Göhringer, Hi for Heyne, M for Matschurek, and W for Weichelt, etc. Luftwaffe pilots detached to fetch a Bf 109 often indulged in extremely low flying, perhaps to impress an 'acquaintance' from the previous evening. Many a red-faced pilot had to land back at Deurne with his propeller – costing RM 9,500 – bent backwards after touching the water of the river Scheldt. On one occasion even the cover for the underwing radiator was missing after a similar 'test flight.'

In order to ensure an adequate supply of skilled workers, a special school was created at Kortrijk, in Flanders, where woodworking craftsmen and by then unemployed diamond workers could be retrained as skilled metal craftsmen. Indeed, the need for skilled workers grew steadily as an increasing number of Bf

Top left: Repaired aircraft were taken by lorry to Antwerp-Deurne airfield from Erla VII.

Bottom left: As in every air force's maintenance depots, defects and remedial results were usually chalked temporarily on some prominent part of an aircraft; in this case the propeller blade. Inscription here reads – 'Motor schüttelt – läuft hoch' – Engine vibrates, idles too fast.

109s were brought in for repair and as the German aircraft industry began ordering sub-assemblies for their own production lines, such as bomb racks for the Focke-Wulf Fw 190 – an item designed by German Erla VII engineers at Mortsel. Another repair depot, Erla VI, was at the same time repairing Messerschmitt Bf 110s and Me 210s, Heinkel He 111s and Dornier Do 217s at Evere airfield, north of Brussels. In May 1942 the first set of plans for the Messerschmitt Me 262 twin-jet arrived at Erla VII, together with an order to prepare for series repair of this revolutionary new aircraft! By early 1943 Erla VII was employed about 3,000 workers at Mortsel, augmented by 400 more at Deurne airfield, and 200 in a workshop set up in a former diamond-cutting establishment in Antwerp's Lamorinière Street, for the diamond-cutting trade had been stopped by the war. From every front wagon-loads of Bf 109s were brought to Mortsel – from within

Above: Most of the Bf 109s were test-flown painted in a light grey (Hellgrau 76) finish, and carrying the first letter of the particular test pilot's surname chalked on the fuselage. The Balkenkreuz and swastika markings were already painted on. Note the pre-war Citroen 'towing tractor'.

Germany, from Russia, even from North Africa with desert sand still lodged in various parts. In addition, arrangements were already in hand to commence similar complete overhaul maintenance for Focke-Wulf Fw 190s, the first of which arrived at Erla VII in the summer of 1943.

By this time Erla VII had become so vital to the German war effort that the decision was made to work day and night continuously, with the work force divided into three shifts. None of this activity went unnoticed by the Allies. Several intelligence rings operating inside Belgium sent regular reports to London on various subjects, including the economic situation, military movements and among other specifications, Erla VII and its activities. Some of the rings conveyed weekly reports, via couriers, by way of neutral Spain. In 1941 the 'Tegal' intelligence ring had been reporting on Erla VII, but when this ring was virtually liquidated by numerous arrests by the Germans, the task of informing London of the activities at Mortsel became the responsibility of the 'Boucle' ring. Two of 'Boucle's' men, known by their code names as 'Ulysse' and 'Le Sage', lived in the immediate vicinity of the Erla works, and with their report of 30 March 1943 they even succeeded in sending plans of the repair depot to London. By then however the Allies had decided to do something about Erla VII and the US 8th Air Force was tasked with the job. Since 17 August 1942, when 12 B-17 'Flying Fortresses' had stepped lightly on the little finger of the German war machine by dropping 18 tons of bombs on the Rouen marshalling yards in France, the 'Mighty Eighth' had gone from strength to strength. As a direct outcome of the Casablanca Conference (14 to 26 January,

1943), Germany's aircraft industry was second on the Allied bombing priority list; only attacks on U-boat yards were deemed more important.

On 4 April 1943, during the daily operations conference at headquarters of the 8th Bomber Command at Daws Hill Lodge, near High Wycombe, Buckinghamshire, the meteorological officer 'promised' only one-tenth cloud over Antwerp for the following day. Texas-born Lieutenant-General Ira Eaker, after staring at the wall map with its many red-ribboned routes to and from various targets, ordered the attack on Erla VII for next day. Field Order No.140, dated 4 April, 1943, supplemented by 1st Wing FO No 126 and 2nd Wing FO No 88, specified the target and ordered the attack for 15.31 hours on 5 April by all available B-17s of 1st Wing and all available B-24s of 2nd Wing. The familiar multi-colour perspective maps were taken from their their secret files and distributed to pilots, navigators and bombardiers; these showed Antwerp as it would look when approached from 26,000 feet. Shortly after 3 pm on 5 April air raid sirens wailed across Antwerp. Streetcars and all other traffic halted; some people went to the air-raid shelters; others simply continued as normal. Reserve Flak-Abteilung 295 (an AA unit), whose six batteries were located around Antwerp, were ordered to 'Alarm' status and their 9cm Flak M39 anti-aircraft guns – captured from the French – were swung towards the west.

At 15.24hrs Flakuntergruppe Antwerpen reported the first enemy aeroplane in sight. Escorted by RAF fighters, 83 Fortress IIs and Liberators belonging to the 44th, 91st, 93rd, 303rd, 305th and 306th Bomb Groups were rapidly nearing the target, spread out in tight

Below: A pair of Bf 109s prior to test-flying. At left can be seen the offices of the pre-1939 Stampe-Vertongen aircraft firm.

Top, right and far right: Erla VII buildings being repaired after the US 8th AF's bombing raid of 5 April, 1943.

Centre, right and far right: Two views of the assembly line at the Rivierenhof plant, where a completely overhauled and repaired Bf 109 was rolled out every hour.

boxes between 23,000 and 26,000ft. Two minutes later the armada was over its IP (Initial Point) at Lokeren, between Ghent and Antwerp, and set a direct course for its objective. In the meantime Fock-Wulf Fw 190s from various *Geschwader* stationed in France and Flanders had been vectored towards the bombers. At the IP a first B-17 was shot down by Oberleutnant Glunz of JG26, though by then Hauptmann Fritz Geisshardt, commander of III./JG26 had already been shot down too.

When the first bombs hit the Erla and Daimler works and fires broke out panic spread among the workers, but thereafter the sticks all fell clear of the works. The results of the raid were disastrous – but not for the Erla works, which was only moderately damaged and even less for the Daimler depot, which was hardly touched. The chief sufferers were the civilian Belgian population in the neighbourhood. Most of the 491,000lb of bombs dropped fell east of the target, towards the built-up centre of Mortsel suburb. Photographs taken during the raid from the bombers showed bombs exploding 5 miles away from the designated target. As the last bombers droned westwards hundreds of civilians lay dead beneath the ruins of their homes, including nearly 100 schoolchildren whose school had been destroyed by direct hits.

The German propaganda machine swung into immediate action. On 11 April Josef Goebbels wrote in his diary: 'An imposing funeral has been arranged by the local authorities for the victims of an American bomb attack on Antwerp. The English and Americans have not yet taken any notice of our propaganda about Antwerp. That is proof of their bad conscience. It supports our idea of making first-class propaganda material of the Antwerp incident.' Of the 79 Fortresses and 25 Liberators that had been despatched, no fewer than 21 had aborted the mission. Three other B-17s were shot down, one each by Oberlautnant Stammberger and Major 'Pips' Priller, and the third by 1./Res. Flak-Abteilung 295. They all belonged to the 306th Bomb Group. After the raid Allied aircraft made several sorties to photograph the damage for assessment. The resulting interpretation reports, drawn up at RAF Medmenham, proved that clearance of the damaged sections of Erla VII was rapidly taken in hand, and much reconstruction had been completed by July that year. On 20 April the 'Boucle' ring reported on the raid. The homes of two of its agents, 'Ulysse' and 'Le Sage', were in ruins, though neither agent was hurt. The report gave the number of civilian casualties as 802 killed and ended by requesting that any future attacks on Erla VII be undertaken by low-flying Mosquito bombers, 'The raid seems to have been performed from too high,' they complained. Only a few weeks after the bombing production was back to normal. Deurne airfield, where at the time of the raid about 50 repaired Bf 109s had been standing, awaiting testing, had not even been scratched by the bombing.

For the remainder of the war Erla VII was unmolested, except for a few sporadic strafings by Allied fighters against Deurne airfield – as on 28 May 1944, when Lieutenant-Colonel

Below: More Bf 109s awaiting flight testing at Deurne airfield, near Antwerp. The hangar was built in the 1920s, and camouflaged by the Germans to look like a row of houses.

Bottom: Some of the civil test pilots of the Erla VII repair depot. The chalked letter F here denoted test pilot Hans Fay, second from left in this quartet./*H Fay*

Robert L Coffey, flying a P-47D Thunderbolt of the 388th Fighter-bomber Squadron, set two parked Bf 109 afire. Many times Erla VII received visitors like Feldmarschall Sperrle, who was furious to discover over 100 Bf 109s parked in the open on Deurne airfield.

From late 1942 all test-flying at Deurne was undertaken with fully armed aircraft, but nevertheless during 1943 an *Alarmstaffel* was created to defend Erla VII in the event of any further raids against the works. Several Bf 109s were always available on the airfield, either waiting for test flights or collection by the Luftwaffe. Now three or four Bf 109s were always kept fully armed and fuelled, dispersed around the field, ready to be manned by the test pilots. To make cold starts easier, the engines' oil was diluted with petrol and during the winter engines were kept constantly warm. On the sound of the alarm the German civilian test pilots immediately became members of the Luftwaffe with military rank, and had to defend the airfield and Erla VII. At first Belgian civilian personnel had been ordered to start the engines when the alarm sounded, but when they protested this order was rescinded.

A few Allied aircraft were shot down by Bf 109s flown by Erla test pilots from Deurne airfield. One was Flight Lieutenant M. Lipinsky of No 315 (Polish) Squadron, who was brought down by Hans Fay on 4 May 1943. Lipinsky was on that occasion flying his Spitfire IX EN131, on a 'Ramrod' mission protecting 8th Air Force bombers attacking the General Motors plant north of Antwerp. He was badly wounded in the leg and had died by the time his parachute reached the ground. On 5 November, 1943, Generalfeldmarschall Erhard Milch sent a letter to Erla VII congratulating the pilots of the Erla-Industrie-Jagerschwarm – Leutnant Göhringer and test pilots Fay and Mörtel – for their victories to date, which comprised one Spitfire and two four-engined bombers.

Even before the bombing raid it had been decided to disperse production at Erla VII. Three quayside hangars from the port of Antwerp were commandeered and, notwithstanding acts of sabotage by members of the Belgian underground, these were erected in the Rivierenhof public park 4km east of the city centre. They were skilfully camouflaged and housed an assembly line that accommodated 54 Bf 109s and produced a totally repaired and overhauled Bf 109 every hour. From that point on test flying was also carried on from Brasschaat airfield, 15km north-east of Antwerp, and occasionally from St Truiden airfield, 70km east-south-east of Antwerp, where Erla VII ran a small repair shop. At the end of May 1943, Betriebsführer (Works Manager) Bartsch could report that no less

than 2,000 aircraft had been repaired by Erla. Telegrams of congratulations poured in, signed by – among others – General Sperrle, Generalingenieur Scheuermann, and General der Flieger Wimmer. Nine months later Bartsch reported to Milch that on 24 February 1944 the 3,000th machine had been repaired since July 1940. Apart from the ever-growing volume of repair work, an increasing number of small sub-assemblies were ordered by German aircraft manufacturers. One example at the end of 1943 was the start of production of a *Rüstsatz* (modification kit) which brought the cockpit ventilation of older variants of Bf 109 to the standard of the Bf 109G-5. The prototype *Rüstsatz* was initially tried and tested by JG 300.

On 6 June 1944 the Allies landed in Normandy, but this did not seem to have unduly alarmed Germans in occupied Belgium. Years later, Bartsch remembered that when he celebrated his birthday on 7 August 1944, there was still no serious thought of leaving Antwerp. Nevertheless, the speed of the Allies' advance through France soon changed this complacent outlook and at the end of August about two-thirds of all machinery at Erla VII was loaded aboard five barges for transport to Germany. Only two barges eventually arrived at Münster, where the firm of L. Hansen was also engaged in repairing Bf 109s. By this time Erla VII was employing nearly 10,000 workers, supervised by a staff of 100 Germans, including men of the *Werkschütz* – a military unit for protection of the installations. Now that liberation was in sight, trouble was experienced with local workers who refused further work and an escalating amount of sabotage was reported. The last remaining Germans only got away in the nick of time when Canadian troops unexpectedly entered Antwerp on 4 September 1944. At Deurne airfield the last two Bf 109s took off as Canadian armoured vehicles rolled on to the airfield. Many 109s had to be abandoned as they were either not fit to fly, or no pilots were available to fly them away. One of the Bf 109s remaining was 'liberated' by some RAF personnel, who occupied the airfield after the Germans had gone, and Squadron Leader Guy Plamondon of 193 Squadron planned to fly it. However, to the dismay of the squadron personnel who had put in many off-duty hours in servicing the aircraft, it was taken away before any flight could be made. Meanwhile the remaining staff of Erla VII had re-assembled at Münster. Near the end of the war Herr Bartsch and others of Erla VII gathered at Leipzig, and on 14 April 1945 were ordered to form a special unit, with some 160 military personnel, to help build Messerschmitt Me 262s. Nothing came of the plan, for the end of the war was only days away.

Defending Neutrality

The Messerschmitt Bf 109s debut in the service of the Swiss Air Force was – to say the least – painful. Wanting to replace its ageing fighters with up-to-date machines, in 1938 the Swiss government ordered the best fighter available at the time – the Bf 109. A series of 10 Jumo 210-engined Bf 109D-1s was available and ready for delivery in November 1938. The first was ferried from Augsburg to Dübendorf by Mani Moser, former chief pilot of the KTA (Kriegstechnische Abteilung). At Dübendorf the *Bise* (local wind) was blowing and when attempting a cross-wind landing the Bf 109 ground looped after touch-down and broke its undercarriage. It took about 100hr (one

working week) to repair the aircraft at Dübendorf. In December one of the next Bf 109s to be ferried was flown by Ernst Wyss, Moser's successor as KTA's chief pilot. Due to heavy snowstorms he was forced to land at Friedrichshafen and continue his flight to Dübendorf next day. A failing engine necessitated a forced landing, with wheels retracted, in the neighbourhood of Frauenfeld. The aircraft was returned to Augsburg by rail for repair, and was ready again in January 1939. On 7 May, 1939, J 314 was ferried from Regensburg to Altenrhein where the A.G. für Dornier-Flugzeuge installed the armament. During the first trial flight on 7 June, flown by

Swiss Bf 109E-3s practising war formations – the necessary 'price' of defending neutrality . . ./ *H Thurnheer (both)*

KTA pilot Oblt Gottfried Suter, loss of engine power caused the aircraft to stall and it crashed into the Bodensee (Lake Constance), killing its pilot. On 24 June, J 322 was delivered but the aircarft crashed near Mollis on 14 July, 1939 after engine failure caused by a broken valve spring. The pilot Lt Wannenmacher was badly injured.

All these accidents gave rise to comments in the Swiss Press, so that in early August 1939, the Eigenössisches Militärdepartment (Swiss Ministry of Defence) saw itself obliged to issue a statement denying assertions published in the press to the effect that the Messerschmitt was a failure and had to be taken out of service. The statement assured that the fighter was up to expectations. Notwithstanding the ominous beginnings, few problems were actually encountered when the Bf 109 was finally introduced into service. Hauptmann Albert Fisher, commander of Fliegerkompanie 8, later to become a director of Swiss Airline, Swissair, remembers:

'The conversion course of my unit at Geneva lasted some two weeks. We first flew the Taifun (Bf 108) to learn the new landing technique. There were very few accidents. The

Morane MS 406 was much more delicate. With the Morane people sometimes bounced hugely on landing, whereas the main risk with the 109 was ground-looping, as the undercarriage track was so narrow. One had to watch it closely when landing. It wasn't difficult – just too new. You had the closed cabin, flaps, retractable undercarriage, different visibility – things like that. The other

Below: Capitain H Thurnheer of Cp Av 6, in front of Bf 109E-3, J-318 of the Swiss Air Force. Note engine starter crank handle in position./ *H Thurnheer*

Bottom: The Bf 109E-3s of Cp Av 6, glistening in the Swiss sun./*H Thurnheer*

Above: Bf 109E-3, J-313 of
Cp Av 6, taxying./H Thurnheer

Left: Under temporary
shelter, this Bf 109E-3 of Cp
Av 6 displays the unit
insigne, a flying witch on a
broomstick./H Thurnheer

85

difficulty was that one had to change the propeller's pitch by hand and its control was similar to a clock. At 12 o'clock you had pitch for take-off; cruising was at 10.30; and when one needed speed, the setting was towards 10. When one forgot to change the pitch setting before landing, one simply didn't touch the ground – one just kept floating. I remember once while landing at Geneva I forgot to change the pitch setting back, and floated the whole length of the airfield. When one realised what was happening one had to open up to full rpm, and with this wrong setting the machine rolled very badly to one side, very low above the ground. Such things did happen, but they were always due to carelessness. One officer in

my Fl. Kp once took off from Interlaken – this was even more stupid – with his propeller at coarse pitch. Like that one simply did not leave the ground. We immediately saw what had happened; but he didn't. Finally he rolled through some undergrowth and fell into the River Lütsche. There were few accidents due to technical faults, but things changed when, in May 1944, we got the Bf 109F. They were a complete failure – very poorly built and clearly sabotaged, probably by non-German labour. We found deliberate faults, foreign bodies here and there, and so on. We had to make one emergency landing after another! The aircraft were even sent for complete overhaul, but it was hopeless as we couldn't get any spare parts.'

Walo Hörning, who from 1938 to 1941 was commander of Fl. Kp 21, and later of Flieger Abteilung 7, recalled one of the rare accidents caused by a technical fault:

'Oberleutnant Victor Streiff, deputy commander of Fl. Kp 21, had an unusual accident during a patrol on 2 January, 1940. He was flying J 312 with his *Sohn* ('son' – wing-man) and they were chasing a Luftwaffe Bf 110 from Dübendorf towards Winterthur below a layer of high fog. They were flying only some 100metres above the ground and 100metres below the fog layer at a speed of about 320 km/h. Suddenly Streiff's Bf 109 became grossly tail-heavy and could not be kept level by pushing the stick forward. As a result it started looping and entered the cloud layer. Streiff quickly threw off the canopy and baled out while the aircraft was on its back. Hanging below his parachute, he heard the 109 complete

GRIM BEAUTY. Bf 109D-1,
J-305 of Fl. Kp 21 silhouetted
against the rugged Alps –
often described as the Roof
of Europe./*A Fischer*

its loop – he could not see it in the clouds –
and immediately afterwards crash into the
ground. Streiff got down safely, though his
parachute only opened fully a few metres
above the earth, and he landed about 500-
metres away from his crashed aircraft. It was
later found that the screw for trimming the
tailplane had come loose from its support and
at the high speed they were flying, the elevator
had taken its fully negative position and
forced the nose of the aircraft upwards.'

One of the first Swiss service pilots to fly a
Bf 109 was Capitaine Hans Thurnheer of
Compagnie d'Aviation 6, a squadron manned
by personnel of the French-speaking region
of Switzerland (though at one period 60 per
cent of its personnel were German-speaking).
His carefully preserved *Carnet de Vol* (log-
book) records that he first flew a Bf 109 at
Dübendorf on 7 January 1940; this was J-301,
the lowest-serialled of the first batch of Jumo
210-engined Bf 109D-1s – or 'Jumos', as the
Swiss pilots called them. His first flight in a
'Daimler' (Bf 109E-3) took place on 6 July,
1939, after some flights in a Bf 108. Thurnheer
recalled:

'We were of course very impressed when
we heard that we were to fly the 109. It was
during January 1939 that we converted at
Dübendorf. We had only one Taifun (Bf 108)
and that was not enough, so Messerschmitt's
chief 108 pilot, Brindlinger, came to Dübendorf with another Taifun with German
registration and wearing a swastika on its tail.
On 4 January, 1939 I flew in HB-HEB (Bf
108B-1, c/n 1988, registered on 27 December,
1938). Then came my first take-off in a Jumo.
I still remember how, when I had at last retracted the undercarriage, set the propeller at
its proper setting and glanced outside, I was
already over Rapperswil (about 20km south-
east of Dübendorf airfield.) One pilot after
another was converted to the new type and we
were mighty proud to be flying such an aircraft – a giant step from our Dewoitine D-27s.

'When we saw contrails for the first time
we were rather alarmed, as at that time we
didn't know what they were. We were frightened when suddenly the leading aircraft
started to "steam". We didn't know where
the "steam-clouds" came from, but then we
did really crazy things like climbing without
pressurised cabins to a height of nearly
11,000 metres (36,000 feet). Making contrails
soon became a sport for us and we made
various figures in the sky. We even had two
specialists who tried to write "CPA 6" (our
unit abbreviation) in the sky above Zürich.
What they "wrote" was unreadable, of course,
but the strange sign in the air prompted a
local Swiss newspaper to write that St
Niklaus von der Flueh, a Swiss saint who had
once lived at Sachseln and still revered by

89

pilgrims, had put his "protective hand above the sinful city of Zürich!"

'The Bf 109Es were delivered by Messerschmitt without armament or radio and only with basic instruments, and when war broke out not all our aircraft had full armament. We regretted that the Oerlikon 20-mm MG FF cannon was installed, as we considered the cannon made by the Schweizerische Waffenfabrik to be better. This had a high initial velocity and its trajectory was much flatter, but it was impossible to instal this type of cannon in the 109. When Germany invaded France on 10 May, 1940 Swiss air space was repeatedly violated by Luftwaffe aircraft, mostly bombers returning from raids on France. On the very first day I engaged a Junkers Ju 88 while flying J-316. I fired some warning shots across its nose, then attacked in earnest when the Junkers' gunners answered my first shots. It disappeared into cloud.

'On 1 June a dozen Heinkel He 111s of KG 55 penetrated Swiss air space and I was one of four 109 pilots who engaged tham above the Jura mountains, flying J-315. When we tried to make them land they fired at us, so we attacked and shot down two without loss to ourselves. This action brought me in front of a court martial, because Germany claimed that we had attacked the bombers over French territory. This was not really the case, but Germany put such heavy pressure on the Swiss Government that it was forced to have the matter investigated by a court martial. It was all very depressing for us, as we honestly believed we had only done our duty.

'But the worst fight was yet to come – on 8 June, 1940. The first losses sustained by the Luftwaffe at the hands of Swiss 109s had already infuriated Göring. Just imagine: German-built fighters from a small, neutral country, flown for the most part by German-speaking pilots – it was too much! Göing ordered sharp measures to be taken: he would teach those Swiss a thing or two. As threats from the German hierarchy had not met with much result, he decided to take steps himself and ordered several formations of Heinkel He 111 bombers to fly intentionally over Switzerland on 4 June, accompanied for the first time by Messerschmitt Bf 110s. The result was that two Bf 110s and one He 111 were shot down, for the loss of one Swiss Bf 109C, J-310.

'Göring's temper rose, and for 8 June he ordered the Swiss to be challenged by a complete *Zerstorergruppe* of Bf 110s operating from Freiburg, only 45km from the Swiss border. At 3.30 in the morning Fl. Kps 6, 15 and 21 were at a state of readiness. A few minutes before noon we were ordered to take off from Thun. Less than 20 minutes later we were over the Jura mountains where we soon spotted the Bf 110s – 32 of them! It

was a spine-chilling sight and even today when I hear the number 110 or see a picture of a 110, I become uneasy. Before we arrived on the scene two 109s of Fl. Kp 15 had engaged the Germans and one 109 had been shot down. This mass of aircraft was flying around in huge circles at three different height levels. We were in no way prepared to attack such a mass of aircraft at that time, and that is why all 12 of us each attacked separately. That was a mistake, because the Germans were well prepared and when we attacked they immediately tried to encircle us. All we could do was try get a 110 in a favourable position for a quick attack – fire, then try to escape as fast as possible. There were various methods of getting away, such as very tight loop – which the 110 could not follow – or half a loop followed by a roll. Anyway it was a rather dangerous situation. as we were alone when we attacked. If we had then had the battle experience we later accumulated, we would have shot down more than the three we managed to get. We had no losses. Hauptmann Homberger was shot through the lungs, but managed to land at Biel. He was also shot in the buttocks, but a good luck charm he was carrying in his purse saved him from further harm!'

Not all Luftwaffe aircraft came over Switzerland with belligerent intentions, however; some simply lost their way. Feldwebel Martin Villing, who in mid-1942 instructed future Luftwaffe fighter pilots in southern France, was one:

'On 12 June, 1942 we were ordered to ferry seven Bf 109s, destined for Africa, from Le Bourget, Paris, where they had been overhauled, to Munich-Riem airfield. Freiburg was to be our first stop. We wanted to paint the town red and each of us had a bottle of cognac aboard to show off, as this was unobtainable in Germany at that time. Obergefreiter Heinrich Scharf and I took off at 5.30 in the afternoon towards Freiburg. Beforehand I had obtained information from the Met Office and calculated our bearings. We climbed to 2,500metres as visibility was good. Everything went according to plan until we arrived in the neighbourhood of Freiburg. We looked for the Rhine without success as there was a thunder storm above the Rhine valley and everything looked black. We could not see the town of Freiburg and gradually our situation became critical as our fuel would only last for another 10minutes. I searched and searched, becoming more nervous all the time. The red warning light started to flicker: it was high time to land. Far away to the right I spotted a large town which I took to be Freiburg. We turned towards it, flying very low over the railway station twice but unable to read which town it was. Then I suddenly saw gliders flying very near. Think-

Right: As in any military service, muscle-power is a constant necessity. Ground crews manhandling a Swiss Bf 109E-3 into its parking area.

Below right: ENFORCED 'GUEST'. Heinkel He 111P (Wk Nr 1905) of the Luftwaffe's KG 55, which was shot down by Bf 109Es of Fl. Kp 15, near Ursins, in May 1940./J P Thevoz

ing that these were German, and reasoning that where there were gliders there must be an airfield, we flew in their direction, soon spotted the airfield and let down our undercarriages to land.

'I was actually landing when I noticed white crosses on the parked aircraft – and suddenly it dawned on me that I was in Switzerland! We had arrived at Bern-Belpmoos airfield. With the last drops of fuel I rolled out after landing, then my engine stopped. Before I had even opened my canopy two Swiss guards motioned me out of the aircraft; they probably feared that I would destroy the machine. My *Rottenflieger* saw it all from above and wanted to fly away, but then his engine started spluttering and he only just managed to land. While he was still rolling the Swiss fired a shot through the aircraft fuselage half a metre behind the cockpit. They later declared that they thought he wanted to take off again.'

A few weeks later the two Germans received company: Alfredo, an Italian pilot who had also lost his bearings. The two Luftwaffe pilots were released on 21 December, 1942 in exchange for Flight Lieutenant Wooll, RAF, who had landed his Mosquito PR IV, DK310, GL-Y at Bern-Belpmoos on 24 August, 1942. The two German aircraft, Bf 109F-4/Zs. remained in their hangar at Bern for the duration of the war. In the summer of 1946 they were given Swiss registrations J-715 and J-716, made one test flight each and were then flown to Emmen, where they were scrapped early in 1947.

Obergefreiter Martin Scharf died when his aircraft crashed at Verneuil, France on 20 June, 1944. Martin Villing ended the war as an *Offiziersanwärter* – officer-candidate – serving with III./JG 5, having obtained 21 accredited victories. When he was finally released as a prisoner of war on 17 June, 1947, one of the first things he did was to meet in Konstanz with one of his former Swiss guards to thank him for his excellent treatment while an internee. Villing then resumed his original trade as a machine mechanic in his birthplace, Stockach, where 33 years later he recalled his adventures.

Far left: UNINVITED. Oberfeldwebel Martin Villing, one of the two Luftwaffe pilots who landed at Bern, Switzerland on 25 July, 1942, in his Bf 109F-4/Z./*M Villing*

Left: 'Enjoying' captivity in Switzerland; from left, Oberfeldwebel Martin Villing; an Italian fighter pilot; and Obergefreiter Scharf, 1942./*M Villing*

Away from War

During WW2, Sweden, like Switzerland, was a haven of neutrality, and occasionally a Bf 109 would 'get lost' and wind up in this neutral country. The months April and May 1945 saw a number of Luftwaffe pilots who did not cherish the idea of becoming prisoners of war, and accordingly sought refuge in Sweden. In all, 13 Bf 109s came down on Swedish soil throughout the war. Any foreign aircraft coming down in Sweden was given an official landing code identity, and it is this code which is mentioned in the first column of the following of the 'lucky 13' Bf 109s.

Left: 'VISITORS' TO SWEDEN. Bf 109s T 75 (nearest) and T 79, both of which landed at Rinkaby; the first on 12 April, 1945, and the second on 24 April, 1945./*B Widfeldt*

Centre, far left and left: T 90 being evaluated by the Swedish Air Force (Flyg Vapnet) at Bromma. It crashed before it could be handed over to the USSR./ *B Widfeldt*

Below: T 90, a Bf 109G (Wk Nr 130297) immediately after landing at Bulltofta on 4 May, 1945./*B Widfeldt*

Above: T 99, a Bf 109G-8, the last to land in Sweden. Balkenkreuz and swastika have been over-painted here; it was handed over to Russia on 8 November, 1945./ *B Widfeldt*

Code	Date	Place	Type	Werke Nr	Remarks
T 17	24 Oct 1940	Karlstadt	E-4	0820	Uffz Ludwig Fröba, 4./JG77; lost way in flight from Trondheim to Oslo. Aircraft brought to SAAB/L for technical survey.
T 25	24 Feb '42	Dorotea	E-4B(?)	?	Radio code KB+LS; pilot deserted; belly-landing. Aircraft possibly returned to Germany.
T 34	24 Aug '43	Glimakra	G-4	?	Pilot lost, baled out, aircraft crashed. Parts sold or scrapped; to Blecker and Co. AB, Malmö, 4 Feb 1944.
T 36	9 Oct '43	Kristianstad	F-2	6741	Landed after navigation error. Radio code DJ+JW. Test flownby SAAB and Fc(SAF test centre.) One cannon taken to Bofors.
T 37	9 Oct '43	Dansjö gard	G	9542	Belly-landed after navigation error. Still in Sweden 1946 at F 12.
T 56	15 Nov '44	Stordalen	G	?	Pilot lost during flight from one base to another in N. Norway; baled out and saved. Aircraft crashed, parts still remain at crash site, 1975. Built by Wiener Neustädter Fluzeugwerke / Avions Caudron.
	17 Nov '44	Kutjaure	G	?	Hgfr Ecke lost during flight from N. Norway to Bodö. Pilot baled and saved; aircraft never salvaged.
T 74	12 Apr' 45	Rinkaby	G-10	77 0261	Landed with fugitive from Berlin area. Aircraft test-flown by Fc.
T 75	12 Apr '45	Rinkaby	G-10	77 0293	Landed with T74, from Berlin area. (C/n also recorded as 77 0093 . . .?)
T 79	24 Apr '45	Rinkaby	G-14	49 0137	Landed with fugitive from Usedom, Baltic area. Testflown in Sweden. (C/n also recorded as 40 9137 . . .?)
T 90	4 May '45	Bulltofta	G	13 0297	Landed after navigation error during flight from Weichsel area. Crashed during test at Bromma Airport, prior to handing over to USSR.
T 98	8 May '45	Bredakra	G-8	?	Landed with fugitive from Kurland. Handed over to USSR on 27 August 1945.
T 99	8 May '45	Bredakra	G-8	?	Landed with fugitive from Kurland. Handed over to USSR on 8 November 1945.

Stalling Speeds and C_L Max.
$W = 5{,}580$ lb. $S = 174$ sq. f.

Condition		Pilot's A.S.I.		Indicated airspeed V_I (from trailing static).		C_L	
Flaps and Ailerons	Undercarriage.	Speed at which Slots open. m.p.h.	Stalling Speed. m.p.h.	Speed at which Slots open. m.p.h.	Stalling Speed. m.p.h.	C_L at which Slots open.	C_L max.
Up	Up	111	75	120.5	95.5	0.865	1.4
Down { Flaps 42.5°	Up	90	61	100.5	81	1.2	1.9
,, { Ailerons 10°	Down	90	61	100.5	81	1.2	1.9

And not only Pilots

SPIT AND POLISH. Ground crews cleaning up the Bf 109F of Oberfeldwebel Johann Pichler of III./JG 77, in Russia./*W Schäfer*

'I first got acquainted with the 109 as a trainee engine inspector, but the episode unfortunately ended with a court-martial. During 1940, II./KG 30, equipped with Junkers Ju A-5s, was stationed at Perleberg, and a Bf 109C-2 from the Werneuchen fighter pilots' school had been sent to Perleberg to be used in air fighting exercises. Its pilot was Oberfeldwebel Gessner. After a few flights shortly before Christmas 1940, the pilot reported the engine as running rough at an approximate height of 300metres. The *Prüfleiter* (head of section) ordered me to find the fault and remedy it. After re-adjusting the carburettor – the Jumo 210 did not have fuel injection – I ordered a test flight and asked the pilot to make a low pass over the airfield so that I could see if the engine still left any smoke trail. He did so, and the engine ran faultlessly. The result, however, was that the head of flying control, a *Major* without flying experience, had the pilot arrested right out of the cockpit for violation of flying discipline! Even when I told him that I had ordered the flight, the well-fed *Major* would not change his mind. The pilot remained detailed over Christmas and the New Year in spite of protests from the civilian personnel in the repair shop, pilots of II./KG 30 and myself – and despite the fact, too, that the pilot was an instructor at Werneuchen. Then events in the west took the pilot to France, where he scored 16 victories in a short time.

'The *Major* still insisted on a court-martial however, and the pilot was brought back from

Left, top to bottom: 'Warte'. 'Warts', or 'Black Men' (from the black overalls usually worn) – the indispensable, hard-working ground crews who provided the essential foundation for all operational flying. These particular airmen served with III./JG 26./*A Weise*

SWEAT AND MUSCLE. The two essential ingredients of good servicing; exemplified here by two 'Warts' of JG 3, 'Udet', working on a Bf 109G-6/E2/Trop 'Pulk-Zerstörer'. Note the Wfr.Gr. 21 mortars under the wings, and spiral nose marking, in black and white./*Bundesarchiv*

Calibrating the engine fuel consumption at Deurne airfield on a Bf 109 repaired at the Erla VII depot (see text).

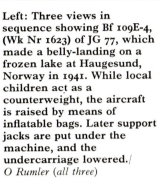

Left: Three views in sequence showing Bf 109E-4, (Wk Nr 1623) of JG 77, which made a belly-landing on a frozen lake at Haugesund, Norway in 1941. While local children act as a counterweight, the aircraft is raised by means of inflatable bags. Later support jacks are put under the machine, and the undercarriage lowered./ O Rumler (all three)

Above: Hauptmann Günther Schack, commander of I./JG 51, explains to his ground crew some defect found during his recent mission./G Schack

Top centre: 'Waffenwarte' – The armourers check over belts of ammunition prior to filling the guns' tanks.

Top, far right: HARMONISATION. Another essential task for the armourers; aligning and adjusting the gun barrels and mountings to ensure all are correctly synchronised in firing. In this case use is being made of a prepared plywood harmonisation disc.

Above right: 'White 9' of III./JG 26 has a change of motor at Caffiers, France in late 1940./A Weise

the front, and myself from the technical school Perleberg. The trial took place in May 1941, but thanks to a sensible judge, to Werner Baumbach as a witness and defendant, and my own technical explanation, the pilot was acquitted. As a civilian I could speak more freely. The Chief Engineer of the RLM kept nodding his approval all the time I spoke at the trial, and this gave me courage to speak out, especially against the *Major* who wanted a conviction at all costs. From then on the *Major* was ignored and despised by all personnel at the airfield. The pilot, later, often forwarded to us a case of French wine, whenever a Junkers Ju 52/3m flew over from France.

'After I had obtained my engine inspector's licence, I was sent to a large Front Repair Shop (*Feldwerft*) at Banak in Norway, to look after KG 26 and KG 30. For a while I had nothing to do with the 109 as no fighters were stationed there. In June 1942 three Russian DB-3 bombers attacked our airfield for the first time. All bombs fell in the water at the edge of the field, but nevertheless three Bf 109E-3s of III./JG 5, stationed at Kirkenes, were then detached to Banak. The Russians did not know of this and attacked next day

with 16 bombers of the DB-3 and Pe-2 types. Most of them were shot down or crashed against the mountains surrounding Porsanger Fjord during the ensuing combat. Only one Russian survived, a snow-white haired major who saved himself by parachute. We treated him decently. He had wrapped his possessions – a family picture and some roubles – in a *Pravda* newspaper. He was shivering with cold – the Arctic ocean is not exactly a sauna – and kept wondering why he was being treated so well. Next day he was taken by Ju 52/3m to General der Flieger Stumpf, commander of Luftflotte 5, whose territory included Norway and Finland.

'One of the 109s had received a hit in the cylinder head cover, but this could be welded on the spot. After this action the 109s were recalled to Kirkenes. During take-off from our *Knüppelstartbahn* (runway of wooden logs) one of the 109s swung off the runway, left the ground, stalled out of the turn and crashed to complete destruction. Yet the pilot was unhurt thanks to the robust construction of the central section of the 109s fuselage and cabin. We engine inspectors had little trouble with the 109 because it was a tough aircraft. Only

Facing page, top left: 'Yellow 4' (Wk Nr 1552) under temporary shelter during routine servicing. JG 26, Caffiers, 1940./*A Weise*

Facing page, top right: Open air servicing on a DB 601 engine – the 'Werft' (repair section) of III./JG 26, Caffiers, 1940./*A Weise*

Facing page, centre left: RE-FUELLING. Adolf Galland's Bf 109E of III./JG 26 has just had its tanks replenished. Caffiers, 1940./*A Weise*

Facing page, centre right: 'Yellow 9' of III./JG 26 undergoing daily engine servicing at Caffiers, 1940. In background is Klemm Kl 35, NR+NN, the unit 'hack' transport aircraft./*A Weise*

Top: An airframe fitter effects a small skin repair on a Bf 109E of III./JG 26 at Caffiers, 1940./*A Weise*

Above: WOMEN AT WORK. The 'fair sex' also helped. Two German civilian helpers working on the DB 605A-1 engine of a Bf 109G-6 at the Messerschmitt Works at Regensburg-Prüfening. As was the custom, defects have been noted, in chalk, on the propeller blade./*Messerschmitt-Archiv*

Left: WAITING, WAITING ... Ground crews taking advantage of a brief pause in their round-the-clock duties to enjoy the sun, next to their 'charge', a Bf 109G-5./*Bundesarchiv*

the airframe inspectors suffered, by reason of the machine's narrow undercarriage.

'I then had to work on Bf 109G-6s, at the Stavanger-Sola airfield in west Norway. Engine cooling during fuel consumption tests always presented a problem. Due to the position of the cooling radiators outside the slipstream, cooling was poor during stationary running of the engine. We solved this by asking the airfield fire brigade to spray water on the cooling radiators so that we could measure fuel consumption accurately. How tough the 109 was can be illustrated by one which crashed after an *alarm* take-off. In his haste the pilot forgot to set the tail trim at its usual position of plus 1 degree. After unsticking, the Bf 109G-6 climbed sharply, stalled and crashed, breaking into three parts. The wings came off, the engine broke loose and the fuselage finished up on its back right next to our repair shop. We lifted the fuselage and from underneath it the pilot, Feldwebel Schulte, crawled from the cabin with only a superficial scratch on his hand. We found the tail trim was still set at minus 6-degrees, thus acting as a full-up elevator.

'A delicate job, and sometimes a problem, was the adjustment of the automatic propeller-pitch setting mechanism. This mechanism was situated on top of the DB 605A (and AS) engine, in front of the double Bosch ZM2 magneto. Any incorrect adjustment could mean an accident, because rpm, boost pressure, propeller pitch and ignition timing all had to be set in harmony. At the front, this adjustment, as well as fuel consumption measurement and adjustment of the Bosch fuel-infection pump, could only be undertaken under the supervision of an engine inspection master (*Triebwerkprüfmeister*). When measuring fuel consumption the exact rpm was found by using a hand-held tachoscope. (I still remember that the tool kit we used for this job carried the number FL Nr 18605.) Mechanics and inspectors in the Luftwaffe then had to have a lot of knowledge about mechanical things, had to be capable of making parts themselves, and had to be able to 'organise' parts – in other words, of scrounging from the *Luftzeugamt*. At Stavanger I had no less than eight reserve DB 605 engines and VDM propellers. The technical officers of the *Staffel* also needed to be very knowledgeable – more so than nowaday when parts are simply replaced.'

Oskar Rumler was private mechanic to Willy Stör, German aerobatics champion of 1935 and 1936, who flew a BFW M35 on those occasions. Apart from working on Bf 109s, Rumler worked on various other aircraft types, including Messerschmitt Me 262 jets. He is now retired, living close to the large Luftwaffe base at Fürstenfeldbruck, near Munich.

In African Skies

COMRADES-IN-ARMS.
Bf 109E-7 of 7./JG 26 taxying
past a Fiat CR 42 of the
Regia Aeronautica; the
latter trestled into flying
position, presumably for a
gun harmonisation
check./*Bundesarchiv*

On 8 November, 1942, four days after Rommel started retreating from El Alamein, British and American forces landed in French North Africa. In order to protect the rear of the Afrika Korps, Generalfeldmarschall Kesselring started flying troops to Tunisia the next day. The skies over Tunisia became yet another battlefield for the Luftwaffe. The first Bf 109s to arrive in Tunisia to fight there were those of JG 53, the famous 'Pik As' (Ace of Spades) *geschwader*. With them came the war correspondents, and one of these, Dr Erhardt Eckert, interviewed some JG 53 pilots for *Der Adler*. He started with the *Kommodore*, Oberstleutnant Günther Freiherr von Maltzahn:

'A large formation of enemy bombers attacked our airfield. When I took off the AA was already firing. I flew in the direction of the American bombers and reached its rear formation over the Gulf of Bizerta. In all there were 36 four-engined Boeing Fortress II bombers, flying in three waves. I attacked frontally the bomber flying left of the right-hand wave. Soon two of its engines stopped and, after my attack, the Boeing started to leave a smoke trail. It turned out of its formation and dived, trying to secape. After we had descended from 6,000 to 400 metres, a man jumped from the aircraft and floated down with his parachute. I made one attack after another, firing with all guns. Until the end the American returned my fire. After 15 minutes' fighting the bomber crashed north-west of Medjez-el-Bab and burned out immediately.'

And here is Hauptmann Friedrich-Karl Müller, commander of I./JG 53:

'I did an *alarm* take-off when some 40 American fighters were coming in our direc-

Top right: Retraction test, the hard way! Ground check on the undercarriage of a Bf 109F-2/Trop of I./JG 27 in North Africa. Wing-tips have been removed, and ground crews serve as a counterweight on the tail./ *Bundesarchiv*

Centre, right and far right: 'ROTTE'. A fighting pair of Bf 109E-4/N Trop from I./JG 27 scouring the Western Desert. An otherwise effective upper camouflage scheme is nullified by reflections and shadow./ *Bundesarchiv (both)*

Right: Bf 109E-7/Trop of I./JG 27, flown by the 'Gruppe' adjutant. Note 300-litre drop tank for extra range under its fuselage./*E Neumann*

Far right: START. Bf 109F-2/Trop of JG 27 revs up before taxying away. The 'Wart' (mechanic) takes away the engine starting handle, though this item was often parked in the cockpit, behind the pilot's seat./ *Bundesarchiv*

Retouching the paintwork on a Bf 109 F-2/Trop of JG 27. Note engine starting handle in position, and aileron mass-balance under far wing./*Bundesarchiv*

tion. First I fought six Spitfires, one of which I shot down. While flying home I saw a gaggle of 40 enemy fighters some 2-3,000 metres away. The Americans didn't spot me. I climbed almost vertically, attacked the first Lightning, and it fell burning after a short burst. I dived to get away from the fire of the other fighters, but they did not react to the loss, so I could get away without further fighting. I had to land quickly as I had no more fuel left. The Lightnings mostly avoid combat. When it comes to it, however, we are always holding a winning hand.'

Oberleutnant Julius Meimberg, Staffel-kapitän of I. and II./JG 2 recalled:

'During the afternoon [of 4 December, 1942] a formation of 12 Boston bombers was reported flying over Mateur. Shortly after we spotted them and chased the gaggle which tried to get home by flying very low. Immediately, a *Schwarm* reached the Americans. One Boston had already been shot down and its smoke was mushrooming when I arrived. The other Bostons now flew even closer together and therefore constituted a considerable fire-power. I soon found myself in a firing position. The Boston's right engine at once started burning, it lost height and crashed into the ground. Next I attacked a Boston flying to my left. While turning I found that five Americans had already been shot down. As more Me's had now arrived, a real bunch gathered behind the Yankees. However, I got another one, my third Boston. It crashed down burning. I could only fire a short burst at a fourth machine as all my ammunition was spent. While flying back I spotted one of the Spitfires. Shooting down the 12 Bostons took only five minutes.'

[In fact, the Allied bombers were British – eleven Bristol Bisley aircraft from 18 Squadron RAF. Their leader, Wing Commander Hugh Gordon Malcolm, DFC, was killed, and later awarded his country's highest honour, a posthumous Victoria Cross. This massacre – some 50-60 Messerschmitts were involved in all – saw the demise of the Bisley as a day bomber, while 18 Squadron was temporarily disbanded and re-equipped to recommence operations on 27 December.]

Oberleutnant Jürgen Harder, *Gruppen-kommandeur* remembered:

'Our infantry reported than an American attack was expected along an important road. At once I started a low-level attack with the *Gruppe*. When we reached the road in question, I gave the order: "To the left – attack!". A wild hunt developed for everything that moved down below – tanks, reconnaissance vehicles, cars, trucks, motor cycles, infantry columns. One *Schwarm* attacked a train on the railway near the road. Without braking, the engineer jumped from

Above: Splendid close-up view as a Bf 109G-6/R2/Trop 'Pulk Zerstörer' of JG 3, Udet, revs its engine prior to take-off. Note Wfr Gr 21 mortar under wing./ *Bundesarchiv*

Left: Armourers rolling a 21-cm Nebelwerfer 42, air-to-air rocket, used by the Bf 109G-6/R2/Trop./ *Bundesarchiv*

Below left: An unusual camouflage pattern on a Bf 109 of 2./JG 77 at Gabes, Tunisia, 1943./ *A Kohler*

Right: One way of keeping the cockpit cool was the use of a beach umbrella, as on this Bf 109F-2/Trop . . ./ *Bundesarchiv*

the locomotive and ran away across the fields. Soon, however, the train stopped as it was badly hit, and the rail line began to climb. Shortly before the end of the road I zoomed upwards to 200metres to see if I had hit a particular vehicle, when there was a loud bang in my cockpit. There was a large hole in the left side window through which the airstream entered. The left side of my face was covered with blood and blood was also flowing from my left hand. The instrument panel was completely destroyed. I called the *Gruppe* by radio: 'Am slightly wounded – flying home.' I flew back without any engine control, but performed a good landing. Shortly after the rest of the *Gruppe* arrived. We had no losses.'

Oberleutnant Fritz Dinger, *Staffelkapitän* recalls:

'My mission was to protect a large freighter that was nearing the Tunisian coast near Bizerta. While circling over the steamship I suddenly noticed a long oil streak on the water that approached in a zig-zag from the enemy side I watched the sky and the suspect oil streak at the same time. Suddenly I recognised the long, dark shape of a submarine that now set course directly towards the freighter and fired two torpedoes. Their wake could be seen clearly. I dived at once and fired at the two torpedoes to warn the ship's crew of their danger. The ship made a rapid turn and got out of the torpedoes' path. I then made three attacks against the enemy submarine which dived quickly. My *Rottenkamerad* and I saw a large oil slick on the water, so the submarine must have been at least badly damaged.'

Von Maltzahn survived the war as an *Oberst* with 68 victories, Müller crashed to his death while landing at Salzwedel on 29 May, 1944, having obtained 140 victories; Meimberg also survived the war as a *Major* with 53 accredited kills. Harder, having become *Kommodore* of JG 11, crashed to his death near Berlin on 17 February, 1945, probably due to lack of oxygen. He had obtained 64 victories, and was one of three Harder brothers – all Luftwaffe fighter pilots – to be killed in action. Dinger was killed on the ground during an air raid in Italy on 27 July 1943. He had scored 67 victories.

A Chronology of early Bf 109 development, drawn up by Dipl Ing Lusser, head of BFW's Project Bureau, on 20 October, 1934.

DiplIng-, Fl-Stabs Ing Christensen was an official of the Technisches Amt of the RLM.

Main Data of the Chronology of the VJ

1. First briefing discussion in Berlin (Christensen – Lusser) *8.3.34*
2. Second discussion in Augsburg (Lucht – Christensen) *21.3.34*
   Detailed definition of task, invitation for submission of tenders.
   Start of the preliminary project.
3. First visual mock-up inspection *11.5.34*
4. Discussion of radiotelegraphy installations (Schwarz II) *12.5.34*
5. Second visual mock-up inspection *29.5.34*
   During this the following items were found missing:

   (1) Dummy engine BMW 15/115
   (2) Automatic system MGC 30
   (3) MG 17
   (4) All radio data
   (5) All Vemag documents
   (6) Reflex sight
   (7) Rolls-Royce data
   (8) Arrangement of instruments requirements

   We were commissioned to test the installation of three machine-guns.
   We were further informed that, for the time being, only water coolers could be used for JUMO 210 and BMW 115.

6. BFW is requesting the following equipment:

   (1) Complete radio apparatus
   (2) Automatic system MGC 30
   (3) Generator and transformer
   (4) MG 17
   (5) Data on high-temperature liquid cooling.

7. Third mock-up inspection. *21., 22.6.34*
   Attended by seven officials from RLM.
   The following new requirements are made:

   (1) View panel in the floor
   (2) Installation of BMW 116
       (no dummies or data available at all)
   (3) Cartridge case collecting box
   (4) Installation of Revie 3 (no data)

   (5) Fundamental alteration of cabin
   (6) Installation of radio apparatus (no data)
   (7) Investigation of different engine mountings
   (8) Accurate mock-up construction of fuel and lubricant system (no data)
   (9) Complete table of accessories

8. Engine mock-up BMW 116 received on *1.7.34*
9. Discussion between Christensen and Lusser concerning the engine. *17.7.34*
10. Discussion between Christensen, Todtleben, Dettinger, Cornelius. *24., 25.7.34*

    (1) MGC 30
    (2) MG 17
    (3) Vemag
    (4) Arrangement of pedals
    (5) Instrument panel
    (6) Radio equipment
    (7) Variable-pitch propellers

11. Discussion between Christensen and Lusser. *24.8.34*

    (1) Submission of our designs for three MG 17
    (2) Controllable airscrew still unresolved, solution possible only in one or two months' time
    (3) Flexible engine suspension has not been decided on by the client
    (4) Radiator questions
    (5) Design of pilot's seat
    (6) Design of balance of controls

12. Mock-up MGC 30 for JUMO received on *2.10.34*
13. Commissioned Göttingen to test horizontal stabilizers and elevators. *6.10.34*
14. Start of the design and construction of a completely new, detailed engineering mock-up VJ in place of the provisional mock-up ordered by Herr Messerschmitt. *–.10.34*
15. Inspection of the engineering mock-up (16 specialists, 16 page report). *16., 17.10.34*

A letter by Udet to Messerschmitt on 4 April, 1941, concerning 25 faults of the Bf 109F which had been mentioned in a telegram from Generalfeldmarschall Kesselring, Commander of Luftflotte II.

Dear Messerschmitt,

Attached to this letter I am sending you a copy of an urgent telegram from General-feldmarschall Kesselring.

I am very surprised that the chief engineer there has waited until today to present these extensive complaints comprising 25 items and I would be very grateful to you – especially in view of the need to fight against pessimism concerning any new model – if you could send me, by return, a telegram with your comments to be forwarded to the front line.

Some of the points raised in the telegram by Kesselring, enclosed by Udet, are:

"In connection with model Bf 109F the following main complaints have been reported to me:

1. On one aircraft the tail-plane complete with tail section was torn off at the fuselage disconnecting point (panel 9). The fuselage disconnecting point was found to be too weak.

2. The external elevator bearing is breaking away and must be reinforced.

3. The bearing flange for the elevator bearing must also be reinforced.

4. The parking brake is completely inadequate. A mere reinforcement of the spring would hardly be sufficient.

5. The pilot's seat is too far to the front. It must also be pointed out that, due to the present position of the seat, a pilot in full flying kit will be unable to move the control column fully backwards and one result of this is that only wheel landings are possible.

6. The breathing tube is too short for pilots of average and above average height.

7. The breathing equipment for high-altitude flying is also inadequate. An additional pressure-oxygen unit is urgently required.

8. Do away with the engine's pannier.

9. The front and rear bolts holding the wing-tip edges deflect and rattle.

10. The ammunition boxes fitted in the wings are loose and have jammed. This was temporarily remedied in the unit by means of wooden blocks fitted underneath, but this does not present a permanent solution.

11. The oil radiator is inadequately secured.

12. A solution of the wing surface deformation problem which since the unit reported adverse flying qualities with a deformed aircraft has also been observed on the right-hand wing.

13. Securing of plating on landing gear, oil radiator and water cooler.

14. Thermostat must be secured more firmly.

15. The welding of aileron horns on aircraft supplied is to be subjected to a test by the unit based on instructions to be issued by the *Generalluftzeugmeister*.

16. The distance between the ribs of the aileron is larger on the model F than on the model E. Due to poor quality stitching the fabric tends to pull out of shape.

17. Tyre wear is extremely high due to the pronounced toe-in, this is particularly noticeable among aircraft using concrete runways where a tyre change is necessary after 20 sorties.

18. The fuel consumption varies considerably for different aircraft, e.g. the aircraft produced by Arado require 70 litres per hour more than others. It is assumed that the aircraft companies will carry out, belatedly, a more thorough tuning of engines.

19. The red fuel warning lamp shows inaccurate readings. It was found that in one case the lamp did not light up until the fuel had dropped to 10 litres, whereas in another case the lamp was observed to light up with 60 litres in the tank.

20. Complaints regarding the automatic propeller system.

21. Cable securing screws on the valve body are too long, so that the cylinder wall is pierced when the screws are tightened. Result: oil running through.

22. Since the 15mm bush and the deep-groove-type radial ball-bearing at the super-charger are frequently being deflected, an order must be given to have the end clearance checked, if possible, after five hours operating time. Within one quarter, 30 superchargers out of 400 have shown such faults and had to be replaced.

23. One unit proposes a higher basic setting of the supercharger to improve high altitude performance.

24. Due to leaking valves there is a relatively high wear of N-engines (which have a life of about 40 hours). This leads to an increased demand for spare engines.

25. Reduced altitude performance was observed with repaired engines. It is assumed that the performance is not re-tested on altitude test stands but merely by recalculation. Random checks seem essential.

I urgently request that the necessary amendment instructions be issued and the required form changes to be made at the *Gruppen* by industrial teams. Withdrawal of aircraft to industrial plants or to air bases situated rearward is unacceptable for military reasons.

Signed Kesselring
Generalfeldmarschall

JOHANNES WIESE

Right: ON THE BUTT. Harmonising the guns of Major Adolf Galland's Bf 109E of III./JG 26, which he commanded, at Caffiers, 1940. The rudder 'score-board' indicates a tally of 67 victories to date./*A Weise*

Below: Hauptmann Jürgen Harder, 'Gruppen-kommandeur' of I./JG 53, stationed in Sicily in the summer of 1943, talking to the armourers replacing the underwing 20-mm cannon of his Bf 109G-6 with Wfr Gr 21. The wing's undermarkings are BS+NA./*Bundesarchiv*

Through the Kommandeur's Eyes

Major Johannes Wiese *Kommandeur* I./JG 52, later Kommodore JG 52; 133 confirmed victories, 75 unconfirmed:

The mission is over and, one sinks into an old armchair in the *Gefechtsstand* (command post) – a pretentious title, perhaps, for a cramped earthen bunker equipped with a few tables, maps, telephones, a stove (if one is lucky). The mission debriefing is over, a cigar has been lit, and slowly the inner tension and excitement is ebbing away. One begins to ask and answer questions about the *Gruppe* and its support, about comrades who are still fighting. And then the *Spiess* (senior non-commissioned officer) is standing to attention at one's elbow, reporting and introducing a new arrival, Leutnant X, who has been transferred to the staff of the *Gruppe*. The Leutnant, tall, in flying kit with the prominent mark of the *Jagdflieger* (fighter pilot) a yellow silken scarf. He stands at attention and reports himself. A handshake and he is brought into the circle of men in the *Gruppenstab*. Where has he come from? How long has he been flying? Has he brought along a new 109? How was the weather? Who flew with him? Has he seen his new quarters? – just some of the questions put to the newcomer. Have you ever been afraid? is the *Kommandeur's* question. Immediately – how could it be otherwise? – the answer is, 'No, Herr Major'.

'Well, that's it for the moment. I welcome you. Take your time getting used to things. Meet the adjutant, Leutnant Plücker, and the signals officer, Oberleutnant X. You'll have to get acquainted with the others yourself. Then we'll see each other again. You can ask me any questions that might arise . . . and think about that one of being afraid!'

Yes . . . if he only knew how often fear jumps at one's throat during combat, when the tracers flash by, overhead, underneath, and at the sides. When the rudder starts fluttering in a tight turn, so tight that the good old 109 can hardly take it without stalling; when the grey flocks of the AA suddenly start to explode all round as if they wanted to transform you – you and nobody else – into a ball of fire, to make the shreds fly around. *Luchhund* (Lying dog) the north-Germans call anyone who keeps saying he isn't frightened. Of course one could have flown on quietly on a steady course, always stolid and upright. But what does one do?

Stick forward, kick the rudder, maximum rpm. Next second one clobbers one's head against the plexiglass canopy as once again the straps aren't tight enough. One pulls out of the too-fast dive without realising properly how one does it. Pull in one's head as far as possible to the left, because there was a fleeting shadow off the left wing. Pull one's machine into a reciprocal course and imagine having just missed the nose of a Red aircraft. One wants only one thing, to make any defensive movement – then, suddenly, everything has meaning and purpose again and – who knows where he came from? – an enemy glides in front of one's gunsight, as if he'd never heard that such a thing could be dangerous. It can only be fractions of a second in which one reacts, sees one's luck, thinks, then uses it! Red nose, red star, big engine, LAGG – at it! 'Tabak 2?' (Tobacco 2 – call-sign). My *Rottenflieger* – forgotten for a second – no, not forgotten – linked by command obedience, drill, expertise, knowing one's machine. Less than 50 metres separate the LAGG in front of me from the hail of gun and cannon fire that now forcibly thunders into the body of the enemy aircraft. Only the time it takes to blink is left to dive underneath it and climb in a steep turn in front of it; just in time to see the machine explode into a thousand pieces. Fear is gone; elation is already over, because the next shadow is sitting beside me.

Change direction again, looking around, then come the words of relief, 'Tabak 1 from Tabak 2. Confirm shooting down. Am behind you.' Only now does one get a 'lift'; only now does one relax a little. We look into each others

Above: Werner Mölders, 'Kommodore' JG 51, at a Russian airfield during summer of 1941. He was the first 'General der Jagdflieger' (General of the Fighter Pilots), but was killed on 22 November, 1941, travelling as a passenger in a Heinkel He 111, on his way to attend Ernst Udet's funeral in Germany./ *W Schäfer*

Below and bottom: Johannes Wiese, 'Kommandeur' of I./JG 52, giving 'fatherly' advice to some junior members . . . !/*J Wiese*

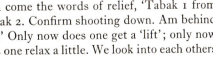

eyes; we wink at each other; see the torch beneath us that lights up on the vast plain – not me, not you, but him. I will ask the new *Leutnant* again how he feels about fear. Before he comes with me on a real combat mission he'll get this question many times. Only when he *knows* fear, *and* knows what to do about it will he go with me – he has to become a fighter pilot on my staff after all – to give us both a chance. It would soon be lost if one could not count upon him being 'with it'; that he has learned how to conquer fear.

We meet again in the evening. 'Seen everything yet? Everything as expected? Talked to the other pilots yet? You might as well have a haircut, then your flying helmet fits better and you sweat less. And you can leave your yellow scarf in your suitcase; we don't fly over the sea here. Is your machine ready? Concern yourself about it; watch closely how it is serviced, it won't do you any harm. And you must become well acquainted with your *Wart* (mechanic). We may have a tour around tomorrow, though not to the Front, to see what you can do.'

'Everything all right?' is the only question I ask next day. I didn't want or need to ask more. I know our mechanics and their conscientious work, but I also know my other pilots who will have told the newcomer more about myself than is perhaps good. I hold a short briefing, pointing out which area we'll be flying in, where the front line is, where they can find the more important recognition points even after an aerial combat, and then; 'Shall we go then'.? We go to our aircraft, strap ourselves in, put on our headsets, put on gloves, give the signal to start the engine, let the inertia starter come to full rpm, pull the starter knob, let the propeller blades get underway and, after checking the magnetos, give more throttle to roll towards the take-off spot. By then I talk to him on the radio, not really in a fatherly way, but at least soothing and encouraging.

Now then, lightly on the brakes – more throttle – a bit more – more – all right – now, up and away. We leave the airfield and are already in the circuit. I position myself in front of him, he beside me, uncertain.

'Well, how are things? Everything all right?'

'Viktor, Viktor'

'Do come a bit closer – still more – more – that's it – all right – easy on the throttle – not so violent with the rudder – relax.'

And so we fly, climbing, getting away from the front line. The sun is already in the west.

'Tabak 2 from Tabak 1 asks Viktor?'

'Tabak 1 from Tabak 2, Viktor'.

When we reach our altitude I let the formation open out, and point out an airstrip below us from where we set course for our own, eastwards.

And then we start to corkscrew about just as

Left, top to bottom: The 44th victory of Oberleutnant 'Tutti' Müller of JG 53 is painted onto his aircraft rudder. He crashed to his death on 29 May, 1944 while landing at Salzwedel airfield./*Bundesarchiv*

Feldmarschall Hermann Göring, Chief of the Luftwaffe, visiting JG 2, 'Richthofen' in November 1940. At his left elbow is Major Helmuth Wick, appointed to command of the 'Geschwader' on 20 November, but killed eight days later. The pilot in the peaked cap is Werner Machold, who had just been promoted from 'Oberfeldwebel' to 'Leutnant'; and who was forced to belly-land at Swanage, Dorset in southern England on 6 June, 1941 and became a prisoner.

JG 52's accommodation at this Rumanian airfield bordered on the primitive . . . /*G Rall*

Pilots of 8./JG 52 breakfast in the open on a Rumanian airfield in August 1941./*G Rall*

Above right: Feldwebel Stefan Litjens of 4./JG 53, greeted by his friends as he vacates the cockpit of his Bf 109E-4 after a mission./ *S Litjens*

Right: MAN'S BEST FRIEND. 'Troll', the pet of Feldwebel Stefan Litjens sitting on his master's Bf 109E-3. Litjens lost his right eye on 11 September, 1941 during combat, but continued to fly operations. On 23 March, 1944, however, his left eye was injured while attacking Allied bombers, thus ending his flying career./*S Litjens*

Below: Leutnant Leykauf of 8./JG 54 (centre) posing with his ground crew in front of his Bf 109E-4, 'Black Three'. The elaborate walking stick here was a fad very much in vogue at the time./*A Weise*

we do over the front line, four, five, six times daily – as one has to do in order to survive. Not elaborately as yet, but in such a way that I soon realise they have sent me a fellow who is already at home in a 109, who can do things with it. I begin risking a bit more, the turns become steeper and steeper while I direct him very cautiously – I don't want to scare him – he still follows. I announce a bunt, which he should copy, clearly hear his 'Viktor' and then roll my 109 on its back. Speed increases rapidly, the 109 starts to whistle, I decrease the throttle a little, see my *Katzcmarek* coming along behind me. 'Well done', I shout, 'Well done, pull the stick slowly, careful, draw in your head, push against the arteries', then in a distorted voice, 'Over quickly, pull out, but follow now'. Seeing black, with blood streaming away from the head into ton-heavy legs, we shoot upwards again. 'Well, had enough? Was it difficult?', I ask Tabak 2.

'Fine,' Tabak 2 replies.

'Very well done', I answer.

I let him take over, position myself on his left wing, don't give him much space to manoeuvre, order him to fly back home. He finds the airfield, lands – him first, after routine instructions – we finish the landing run, stop engines, he comes to me and reports himself as returned.

I ask, 'Well, were you frightened?'.

'No, Major', is his reply.

'Well done, well done as a start. Tomorrow we'll do it again, a little bit harder. And always – *Holzauge sei wachsam*! (Keep looking around).'

In this way we often fly around behind the front line, and I demand more from him in flying skill. He continues to tell me he isn't frightened; he knows my question by now but remains adamant – well, that's his business. Several times he has flown missions but without any contact with the enemy. We have flown across the lines on the deck, looking for enemy aircraft, but nothing has happened. Today, we have taken off to some *Freie Jagd* – free hunting – and show ourselves low over the lines. With 500 on the clock we roar over the heads of our panzermen, infantry and artillery, then head deep into enemy territory. There they are! Six black dots detach themselves from the easterly horizon and come directly towards the German lines. Probably *Hanni* 500 (Hanni – height). '*Pauke, Pauke!* Attack! I'll cover you'. This will be the first break for the new boy. 'Calm now, calm. Take the first one from below – not yet – a bit to the right – not yet – like that – NOW!' Nothing happens, we pass by. The IL-2's have spotted us. The bombs tumble from their bays into the Russian lines – we've reached them at the right moment. They're already forming a defensive circle, no fighter escort to be seen. 'Tabak 2'

Top: The 'Liegeplatz' (accommodation) of Stab/JG 26 at Caffiers, 1940. Note the impressed Citroen car./A Weise

Above: Pilots of III./JG 26 at Vendeville, France in September 1943, in typical Luftwaffe operational fighter pilot garb./A Weise

follows my instructions for a new attack. I direct and correct his approach – now in the enemy circle. Again he gets behind an IL-2, then banks away without firing his guns. I then shoot down the first one, and soon get behind a second, so near that I close my eyes. He explodes in mid-air.

'Careful, Tabak 2. Attack again'. I'm above the defensive circle and again manoeuvre my *Rottenflieger* into an attacking position. He is not at all clumsy. He gets within firing range – now, at last his first one should go down, but again he banks away with no visible result. Immediately, I get lower and come between two enemy machines, dive a little, fire into the radiator, get away underneath it and out in a right turn, find a fourth in front of me and send a volley into the middle of its fuselage. She noses over and breaks apart, spewing flames. The two remaining have opened their throttles and dive away east. I can still see the rear gunner of the fifth one getting larger and larger. His tracers fly close to my nose. But will it help you? You or me, to the death. A hare in his form cannot press any closer to earth than me in my crate. Even today I duck my head, decades after this combat, and sweat maybe more now when writing this account than in my 109 then! Hard hit, the Stormovik crashes into the ground. I came so close to him that my machine bucked and

vibrated. If I remain below, arrive underneath it, then . . . A few touches with the rudder and I'm there, and wham-wham . . . nothing else. By God, I've used all my ammo! And my young friend? He floats beside me but I'll not order him to attack. The sixth Russian flies east, trailing black smoke but we can't chase it. With full throttle we roar towards our own lines. 'Down', I yell in the microphone, 'Down'. My *Rottenflieger* hears the warning and goes much lower than me.

Fliers' luck sees to it that we aren't hit by those small, small bullets from the infantry. It was lucky that we had flown over the German lines before and shown ourselves. At least no fire from our own lines greet us. After a few anxious minutes we climb. To the east we can see five dark mushrooms, five victories, each in front of our own lines . . . When we get back I waggle my wings and do a few rolls so that those below know what has happened. After landing we stop engines and walk towards each other. I hear the *Leutnant* report, 'Back from flight against the enemy.' I step past him towards his machine, step up onto the wing, grip the gun switch, and find it is not switched on. '*Mensch* . . .' is all I can say.

After a moment I call him to me and ask, 'Well? . . .'

Unwaveringly the answer comes, 'Yes, Major, I was afraid.'

112

Right: Oberleutnant Horten explains a point about the harmonisation pattern board to a colleague./*A Weise*

Below: Belly-landing by 'White Seven' of 7./JG 26 at Caffiers, 1940; illustrating graphically the normal rupture point for a Bf 109's fuselage if it crashed or landed too heavily./*A Weise*

In Latin Hands

Above: The defence of Rome was assigned to the 3° Stormo of the Regia Aeronautica, and one unit of that formation was the 7ª Squadriglia. Seen here at Cerveteri, Italy in July 1943 are Bf 109G-6s of this squadron, though other types used by 7ª included Macchi MC 202s, Macchi MC 205s and even a few Ambrosini SAI 207s./G Ghergo

Far left: A Bf 109G of the 3° Gruppo Caccia at Comiso, Italy, 10 July 1943. Just discernible above the exhaust pipes is the devil's head insigne; badge of 6° Stormo, to which 3° Gruppo belonged./G Ghergo

Left: Italian ground crews grouped in front of a Bf 109G-6 of the 7ª Squadriglia, Cerveteri, Italy, July 1943./G Ghergo

Below left: Bf 109G-6 of 364 Squadriglia (150° Gruppo).

Just Routine Testing

The man who has flown the highest number of different Bf 109s must surely be Flugkapitän Wendelin Trenkle. He cannot remember precisely how many, but it must have been several thousands. After leaving high school, he started learning to fly at the DVS (Deutsche Verkehrsfliegerschule) in 1931, and soon obtained various flying licences, including seaplanes, and then flew as a co-pilot with Lufthansa. In 1933 he was one of the German pilots who, in secret, were given a fighter course of instruction in Italy; after which he was appointed as an instructor with the DVS at Schleissheim. Later, while still a civilian, he instructed at various Luftwaffe airfields. Finally he went to work for Messerschmitt, as chief pilot and head of the flying department of the new Messerschmitt plant at Regensburg, which was officially inaugurated on 20 March, 1937. On average he had some 20 pilots working under him, whose job was to test-fly every aircraft produced at Regensburg before it was

Left: Flugkapitän Wendelin Trenkle who tested several thousand Bf 109s./*K Schnittke*

Below: During take-off, the engine of CD+WV tore itself loose . . ./*K Schnittke*

turned over to the Luftwaffe. For a Bf 109 such a test-flight normally lasted about half an hour. Other duties included ferry flights and test flights at auxiliary airfields. From his total of about 15,000 flying hours; roughly 9,000 were flown in the service of Messerschmitt, of which 5,000 were flown in testing new Bf 109s of every possible version. An idea of the scale of this routine test flying is the fact that during the month of August 1944 alone no less than 750 Bf 109s were tested by the Regensburg team.

One of those test pilots was Heinz Frensdorff. Eighteen years old when he first learned to fly at the Reichssportfliegerschule (German Sport-flying School) at Rangsdorf, near Berlin, he soon became an auxiliary flying instructor; then joined the Flettner Aircraft Company at Berlin-Johannistall. In 1943 he joined the team at Regensburg – and lived through some hair-raising moments. He took up a Bf 109G for the first time but had to divert to the much larger airfield at Niedertraubling after the aircraft flaps refused to lower. Trenkle sent him to the Wiener Neustadt airfield for a month's practice on Bf 109s. Back again at Regensburg, his second flight also almost ended in disaster. Test flying BE+WP at about 5,000 metres, one of the engine connecting rods broke, and within seconds the windshield and canopy were covered in oil. Frensdorff tried to bale out but found the canopy was stuck tight. Again, by radio, he was diverted to Niedertraubling where he succeeded in making a wheels-up

landing. For some months than all went well – until he took up CD+WV. During the take-off at full revs, the engine tore itself loose and the spinning propeller made it cartwheel across the airfield before it finally came to rest in a field a kilometre away. The Bf 109 fuselage promptly ground-looped, but again Frensdorff was unhurt, although very shaken. As every flying accident was duly photographed, this 'incident' was no exception. Frensdorff was able to get negatives of some of the classified photographs through the help of a young Hungarian girl who worked in the Messerschmitt photo laboratory, and took the negatives to a camera shop in Regensburg for development. When he went to collect them, however, it took an awful lot of explaining to avoid being brought to trial! The Gestapo, suspecting espionage, were waiting for him...!

Below and bottom: The canopy was stuck, so Frensdorff belly-landed BE+WP at Niedertraubling; his windshield and canopy covered with oil./ *K Schnittke (both)*

Defending the Reich

Return from a mission, with the traditional low beat-up, accompanied by a wing-waggle if any victories were achieved./*G Rall*

Feldwebel Richard Heemsoth wrote the following account, which was published in *SIGNAL*, August 1944. Only a few weeks later, on 11 September, Heemsoth crashed to his death six km north-east of Burghofen/Eschwege:

'That night I had already shot down two enemies and was in great form when I spotted the third one. He was right in my gunsight. I pushed the button . . . wham . . . wham . . . wham it went, then it became silent. My cannon had ceased to fire. I continued firing with the machine guns, but surely with these alone I would not be able to send down this four-engined bomber. The rear gunner of the

bomber must have been killed instantly because his machine guns were silent. I came a little closer, fired again until the last of my ammunition had gone. What now? I was 20 metres behind the bomber which made the craziest turns and tried to get away in the dark. The only thing I could still do was to ram him. Slowly I came closer. It was difficult to keep the aircraft steady in his slipstream but I succeeded. My propeller crashed into the Englishman's rudder. It was a real buzz-saw. It cut through the rudder and tore it to shreds. The Englishman zoomed downwards; my own machine went out of control and I was thrown out. While floating down with my parachute I lost the bomber in the darkness. Then

Supply Drops by Bf 109s

16 March, 1945	16 x 109s	Dropped 2.4 tons ammunition
20 March, 1945	14 x 109s	Dropped 2.1 tons ammunition
22 March, 1945	6 x 109s	Dropped 0.9 tons ammunition
23 March, 1945	8 x 109s	Dropped 1.2 tons ammunition
4 April, 1945	21 x 109s	Dropped 3.55 tons ammunition
10 April, 1945	12 x 109s	Dropped 1.85 tons ammunition
12 April, 1945	16 x 109s	Dropped 3 light field howitzers, & one infantry gun.
13 April, 1945	11 x 109s	Dropped 1.44 tons ammunition
14 April, 1945	16 x 109s	Dropped 3.38 tons ammunition
15 April, 1945	18 x 109s	Dropped 3.18 tons ammunition
16 April, 1945	16 x 109s	Dropped 2.66 tons ammunition
21 April, 1945	7 x 109s	Dropped 1.05 tons ammunition
22 April, 1945	10 x 109s	Dropped 1.50 tons ammunition
26 April, 1945	9 x 109s	Dropped 1.35 tons ammunition

suddenly I saw a great fire-glow down below. It had spattered with its bombs in a meadow. I came down not far away, and a quarter of an hour later I stood near the widely-scattered pieces of wreckage, near a large crater in the ground . . . somewhat further away some cows stood lowing . . .'

Oberfeldwebel Arnold Döring, originally a bomber pilot with III./KG 55, took a conversion course to fighters at Altenburg/Thuringia after completing 348 bomber missions. He then joined JG 300, and his first night mission came on 9 September, 1943:
'There is a new moon, pitch-dark, but glorious weather. Our advance warning system has detected indications of a mission by the Tommies; all nightfighting units are in the highest state of readiness. Ready and all dressed up, we wait in the bus to be driven to the machines standing ready in the take-off area. Into the machines, strap-up, instruments checked with a darkened torchlight. The first 'Wart' helps us. Canopy shut, eyes closed to get acclimatised to the darkness. There, two green Very lights from the *Gefechtsstand* – order to take-off. The 'Wart' who has been sitting on the wing is already cranking away like mad, because it is his pride that his pilot will be the first to take off. '*Frei*' (Free), the 'black man' shouts. I pull the starter, open up the throttle and the engine catches with a crackle. Canopy open, the *Wart* places the starting handle behind in the luggage locker, canopy closed, locked, throttle slowly fully opened, test brakes. Yes, everything's OK. Throttle closed, wheel chocks away, position lights on so that nobody is dragged along. A shadow scurries by and exhaust flames and scattering sparks tell me that a machine has just taken off diagonally. That can only be wild Schäfer who is often up to such pranks. Then I am ready for take-off. I align the bird, open the throttle fully and am soon swallowed by darkness. Undercarriage and flaps up, position lights off . . .
'I adjust my radio and the voice of the ground controller comes through clearly, "Wilde Saue to the Leuchtfeuer Ludwig.* Four-engined enemy bombers over the mouth of the River Scheldt, Hanni 6,000, course towards the east." I fly on course and slowly gain height. I have time and reach the beacon Ludwig before the Tommy. What city will he attack tonight? Will he turn towards the Ruhr area? Will he attack Bremen, Hanover, Berlin? "From Gefechtsstand Heuberg. This is the situation in the air. Dicke Autos in map reference XY, Hanni still 6,000, course towards the east. Out" – The quiet voice of the

speaker from the divisional command post which has now taken over control comes through loudly. I compare my position with that of the Tommies; I should meet the tip of the enemy formation over beacon Ludwig.
"Four-engined heavy bombers now at map reference XX, stretched out, height 4,500 to 6,500, course eastwards. Out. Out."
'The Tommy comes near the Reich's border, the night fighter units from Holland, Belgium and northern France have probably broken up the stream. But still he keeps to the same course, approximately towards Hanover-Berlin. A light flashes intermittently in front of me; . – . . , . – . . ; the Ludwig light beacon. A large searchlight also moves around.
"All Wilde Saue to Bremen, all Wilde Saue to Bremen."
'What's this? The situation isn't clear. I have a funny feeling that something isn't right, so I stay in the vicinity of Ludwig, and soon the order comes through to set course for Berlin. I wasn't wrong after all.
'Searchlights flare up in front, flashes of light make me presume AA fire, it must be Hanover. I fly along the southern border of this AA area, and a few times I have to grab my Very pistol because some AA bursts are dangerously close. Down below my signals are recognised and the firing stops. Even so something must be the matter in this area. I turn towards the north, and fly around Hanover, but not a target is to be seen in the searchlight cones. A new situation report signals the enemy formation near Hanover, also to the north and south of it. Nevertheless, the order still stands to set course towards Berlin. One last turn and I fly east towards the Reich's capital. There, in front of me, red ground markers! For the first time I see this fire-marvel, the "Christmas Tree" lights which the Tommy uses for destruction of German cities, cascading down so slowly. They look beautiful . . . horribly beautiful. Searchlights flash up, flak fires, cascade after cascade, in between illumination, bombs and phosphorous. It must be Brünswick, and immediately I report my observations to Heuberg. They acknowledge, but then over Hanover the real magic starts behind me. Brunswick was only a diversion! Full throttle back to Hanover. Blood-red fires in front of me, then light red, pink to yellow. Hanover is burning. Innumerable phosphorous (incendiary) containers will already have been dropped on the unfortunate city. All around I see aerial combats, the tracers darting back and forth. I see fires starting and quickly becoming larger, then a four-engined bomber falls towards the earth like a torch and ends in a violent explosion as it impacts. I almost ram one of these black monsters when we fly straight at each other. Suddenly his shadow looms ahead; incredi-

Major Günther Rall, recovering after his left thumb had been shot away by an 8th Air Force Thunderbolt over Germany. In all, Rall was shot down five times, but survived the war with 275 accredited victories./*G Rall*

---

*Ludwig: code name for a radio beacon situated near Lake Dümmer.

bly quickly it becomes larger and I can barely haul back on the stick and zoom over it, a hair's breadth away. Where there's one, there must be more.

'By watching the fragmentation bombs detonating below I can figure out the direction of the attack, and position myself across the approach path, constantly curving about. I watch an aerial combat below me ending in a victory. At last I spot an enemy to the right, in front of me, but before I can reach him he is ablaze – one of my colleagues was quicker than me. The same thing happens again, several times. Once I was about to open fire when I spot another 109 quietly destroying my bomber. Go to blazes then, I'm angry now. Another one is attacked by a comrade flying behind me. His bursts swish by right above my canopy and I only just manage to dive away. Way below it has got lighter, an enormous fire-cloud hangs over the burning city. Above it there is an uninterrupted barrage of AA fire, and higher still is the hunting ground of the Wild Boars and the heavy night fighters. Suddenly I see a large shadow above me, I open the throttle wide and the engine roars. I climb and position myself behind the Lancaster. This one *must* be mine – nobody is going to steal it from me! Nerves are taut. He should have seen me long before as I'm silhouetted against a light background. So, higher, exactly behind him, waiting until the twisting Tommy flies steady for a moment. Unfortunately I cannot get him before he drops his bombs, but to do this he has to fly straight and steady, and at the exact moment his eggs leave their racks, I let him have it. The rear gunner must be hit – not a shot comes from there. At 50 metres I continue firing and see my tracers bite into the fuselage and wings; see how finally the wing catches fire between the engines, and then how my victim dives steeply. The fire spreads, the wing tears away, the fate of the Lancaster is sealed. Lit up by three searchlights, it spins down and crashes on the southern edge of Hanover with a huge explosion. I yell "Horrido", and receive confirmations from several comrades, but then am startled when I see the red light blinking. This brings me back to reality – I only have fuel for 20 minutes left.

'I give up the hunt, throttle back, and call until finally a beacon answers and gives me a course and duration of flight to the nearest airfield. It's not easy – 30 other "Wild Boars" also need to land quickly and want directions to the nearest field. My fuel will be just enough to get me there. At last, after a few frightening minutes when the fuel gauges begin registering zero, a row of lamps appear in front; Rotenburg airfield, east of Bremen. The field is brightly lit. I lower the undercarriage, nip in

front of a Ju 88, quickly put on my spot-light and land, closely followed by the Ju 88. The engine coughs – the earth has me back again. Just before I could reach the refuelling point the engine stops. I feel rather upset. It is uncomfortable to realise that my engine could have stopped at any minute while on finals. At least there would have been no explosion when I crashed! I have been lucky again. I get out, peel off my flying suit and stroll towards the airfield control where many crews are already gathered. Among them are some familiar faces; nearly all report victories. My *Staffelkapitän* has got three, our adjutant one, and I report mine. Congratulations from all sides. By telephone I report my success to our own

Top, left and right: Instead of graceful gliders, Wolf Hirth's factory at Nabern/Teck made wooden tailplanes for Bf 109s./ *Wolf Hirth* (both)

Above: A Bf 109G-6 of III./JG 26, flown by the 'Gruppen' adjutant, in September 1943 when the unit was part of the German defence network in France and other occupied countries. JG 26 was disbanded in March 1945./ *A Weise*

Dusk . . . and a Bf 109E-1 of
I./JG 20 (later VII./JG 51). /W Schäfer

command post at Hangelar, then we are invited to a substantial meal at the Casino.

'The Fatherland cares touchingly for the welfare of us "Wild Boars", the youngest branch of the German night fighters. We are called *Herrmannflieger* (Herrmann's pilots – after Major Hajo Herrmann, originator of the *Wilde Saue* tactics), suicide pilots – even death pilots. Indeed many comrades have crashed already as we have only one engine, and many more will crash. But we do have some advantages. We offer a smaller target for the enemy; have more speed and manoeuvrability; which makes a difference. Nevertheless, this kind of flying is not easy; the drawbacks are obvious – the undercarriage is weak; endurance and range too small; only one engine; no radar; no crew, like a wireless operator or navigator. Every mission causes many wrecks to be scattered on the airfields – there are dead and wounded. Still, the list of our successes grows with every mission.'

Arnold Döring survived the war, rising to *Leutnant* and being credited with 23 victories.

Because of the acute shortage of aircraft, the "Wild Boar" night-fighter pilots often had to use fighters normally used by day-fighter units. The units using these *Wilde Saue* tactics – JG 300, JG 301 and JG 302 – suffered such high losses that at the end of 1943 they were reconverted to day fighter units. Oberfeldwebel Stefan Litjens, who finally accumulated a score of 38 victories, lost his left eye on 11 September, 1941 while attacking a Russian bomber. His injury did not prevent him becoming a successful Reich defender.

'On 23 March, 1944 we were stationed at Eschborn, near Frankfurt, as part of the defence of the Reich, We took off at 0907 hours to tackle approaching American four-engined bombers on their way to Berlin. At a height of about 8,000 metres we reached the enemy formation which consisted of several groups of more than 100 bombers. An attack on such a compact formation was a risky undertaking when you consider that in order to ensure hitting them you have to close to 100 metres. During this attack I received several hits from the defending gunners. My intact eye was injured, and I had to break off my attack as I was almost blind.'

During the last months of the war the word *Reichsverteidigung* (Defence of the Reich) acquired a peculiar meaning for certain Bf 109 pilots. In some cases the Bf 109 was used . . . as a transport aircraft! From 15 February, 1945, Breslau, capital of Silesia (now Wroclaw, Poland) had been surrounded by the Red Army. While the siege lasted – until 6 May – the task of supplying the town with arms and ammunition was given to the Luftwaffe. In the main Junkers 52/3ms and Heinkel He 111s were used, plus some Gotha Go 242 and DFS

Above: In Burbank, California, some of the Bf 109's deadliest opponents, the Lockheed P-38 Lightnings were being mass-produced in the open ... / *Lockheed Company*

Right: ... and at San Diego, Consolidated B-24 Liberators, soon to be droning over the Reich, were rolling off the never-ceasing production line./ *Consolidated Coy.*

230 gliders; but Bf 109s were also used to drop supplies in. The War Diary of Luftflotte 6 mentions the drops by Bf 109s given in the table on page 119.

After Berlin had been surrounded by Russian forces it became necessary to supply that city by air too. At first light on 26 April a large formation of Bf 109s dropped jettisonable supply containers over the devastated city centre, but only about one-fifth of these could be retrieved among the ruins. It was during this same period that the doubtful distinction of being the first Luftwaffe pilot to be retrieved by a Luftwaffe helicopter fell to a Bf 109 pilot. In the morning of 6 March, 1945, a Bf 109 pilot of 1, NAG. 4 had lost his way in a snowstorm, and made an emergency landing near the Danzig-Praust airfield. A Focke-Achgelis Fa 223E-0, GW+PA (*WN* 22300051), piloted by Leutnant Gerstenhauer, had been ordered by Hilter to fly to Danzig (now Gdansk, Poland), and it took off to search for the missing pilot. The helicopter finally found him near Goschin, where the injured man was taken aboard and flown to the airfield.

At the E'Stellen

The first prototype Bf 109 spent its first New Year halfway between Berlin and Rostock. There amidst the north-German plains of the former Gau Mecklenburg lies Lake Müritz, and beside the lake, an airfield – Rechlin. During World War 1 this airfield had been used for testing aircraft, and from 1925 military aircraft were secretly tested there; despite the strict ban imposed by the Versailles Treaty. To camouflage the activities at Rechlin the base was titled somewhat ponderously Erprobungsstelle Rechlin des Reichsverbandes der deutschen Luftfahrtindustrie – literally, Rechlin Testing Site of the Reich Organisation of the German Aircraft Industry. The German navy had its own testing facility from 1928, when the former Caspar Flugzeugwerke works was bought and converted into the Seeflugzeug-Erprobungsstelle Travemünde; which was later titled – for security reasons – Erprobungsstelle Travemünde des Reichsvebandes der Deutschen Luftfahrtindustrie – Travemünde being near Lübeck, on the Baltic Sea. When in 1933 aviation in Germany was reorganised, both testing stations were taken over by the RLM and each became an Erprobungsstelle der Luftwaffe; generally referred to as E'Stelle Rechlin and E'Stelle Travemünde. At the end of 1936 a special section of the Travemünde centre developed into a separate testing establishment for all kinds of armament used by the Luftwaffe, and became titled E'Stelle Tarnewitz – Tarnewitz being near Wismar, 40km east of Travemünde.

Before this however another E'Stelle had been planned in a rather desolate region near the small fishing village of Peenemünde, which had been discovered by Professor Wernher von Braun about Christmas 1935. Eventually two testing centres were built here; one for the Luftwaffe, Peenemünde-West, which bordered on Peenemünde-Nord, used by the German Army. During the war more E'Stellen were established at Gotenhafen, Werneuchen and Udetfeld, an airfield in Silesia named after Ernst Udet, the Luftwaffe's GL (*Generalluftzeugmeister*: Chief of Aircraft Procurement and Supply). For some time Erprobungs-Kommandos (testing detachments) were even set up outside of Germany, like at Cazaux, France, Foggia, Italy; and Bengasi, Libya. Thousands of tests and trials were performed at the E'Stellen, and each was the subject of a secret report with a limited circulation. Representative tests involving the Bf 109 included, Erprobung Nummer 2574 at E'Stelle Rechlin; a test whereby the improvement in performance of a Bf 109E was measured when GM-1 Stoff (carried in liquid form under pressure in a cylindrical container behind the cockpit) was injected into the engine's supercharger by compressed air. GM-1 Stoff was the ultimate code-name for N20 – nitrous oxide; – previously coded as HA-HA, but often referred to as *Göring-Mischung* (Göring blend). The report was dated 2 December, 1940. Flying with 2,400 rpm but with varying propeller pitch settings the use of GM-1 Stoff gave an increase in true air speed of between 60 and 105km/hr at heights ranging from 8,000 to 11,000 metres; while between 8,000 and 10,000 metres the climbing speed was improved by two to three metres per second. During the initial flights a periodical improvement and decrease in performance was noted, due to impurities in the gas used. These impurities partly blocked the nozzle until blown away, and was dealt with by improving the manufacture of the gas, and by use of filters while tanking and in the piping system.

Another Bf 109 experiment was fitting a fixed ski undercarriage to a Bf 109E-8. To ensure availability of snow, the Gardemoen airfield, 30km north of Oslo, was chosen for the tests. Dipl Ing Kloppe was appointed as supervisor for the experiment, while the test-pilot from Rechlin was Hans Fay during the 1940-41 winter. Fay had been inducted in the Luftwaffe on 23 July, 1939 and given a flying instructor's course. When war started he served with JG 53 'Pik As' until May 1940, and was then transferred to Rechlin as a test pilot and engineer. There his main job was to evaluate captured aircraft, mainly fighters, of British, French, Russian and American origin. Later in the war Fay became an acceptance test pilot at the Antwerp Erla Repair Depot; while on 30 March, 1945 he flew a Messerschmitt Me 262 intact to the Rhein/Main

airfield. It was established that the fixed ski-undercarriage reduced a Bf 109's performance by about 10 per cent. When all the tests required to establish changes in performance and handling qualities had been completed, a number of flights – so-called *Dauererprobung* (endurance tests) – were made to see how many take-offs and landings could be made before any technical fault developed. On the particular day 37 take-offs had already been made, with an outside ground temperature of −24°C. Thirty five years later Fay still remembered what happened on the 38th flight:

'I was coming in for a landing and was on finals. The sun, at my back, suddenly cast a shadow of the ski-equipped 109 onto the white runway. I noticed suddenly that the shadow cast by the left ski was much longer than that of the right ski. One of the two attachments must have broken or become loose and the ski was hanging vertically! At the same time I saw some mechanics fire a red Very light. It had been decided beforehand that if any serious trouble developed in flight I was to bale out rather than attempt a landing. I climbed back up to 3,500 metres where I baled out. Below me were nothing but woods, and in these the abandoned 109 was later found, totally wrecked. We only learned later that it crashed near a very large ammunition depot!' After this crash the ski-experiment was abandoned.

The E'Stellen also had the responsibility for drawing up the *Kennblatt* (Technical Notes), giving exact description, measure-

WL-IGKS, a Bf 109E-1, being tested in the wind tunnel at the DFL (Deutsche Forschungsanstalt für Luftfahrt) at Braunschweig-Völkenrode, 1941.

ments, armament, equipment, performance, operational limits etc for each Luftwaffe aircraft variant. An example is the report for *Auftrag* (Work Order) E2-48/7, compiled by E'Stelle Travemunde on 23 December, 1941 – the *Kennblatt* for the Bf 109 T-2. The T-2 variant was a development of the T-1, and essentially a Bf 109E-1 adapted for use on the German Navy aircraft carriers *Graf Zeppelin* and *Peter Strasser* that were being built at that time. In the event, the T-2, minus arrester hook or catapult points, saw some service in Norway. The report – *Geheime Kommandosache* 556/41 – consisted of eight pages of text, one page of photographs, and one page with a three-view GA drawing; only 37 copies were printed.

Auftrag E6 19201/42 IIF, which resulted in Report No. 112/41 by the E'Stelle Tarnewitz of 2 September, 1942, dealt with the installation of a pair of MG 151/20 cannon in under wing gondolas on a Bf 109-F4. The aircraft had been modified by the Messerschmitt Augsburg works and equipped with the necessary field conversion kits, but due to bad weather conditions the aircraft could not be flown to Tarnewitz. The prototype conversion kit was sent by rail to Tarnewitz where it was installed in *WN* 7449. First firings showed so many jams and stoppages that the cannon were removed and tested in a firing jig to cure the causes of the stoppages. When, on 24 March, 1942, the first air firing test was made, further stoppages occurred; and only

Left and above: Test Number 2574 at Rechlin; injecting GM-1 Stoff into the engine's intake. First photo shows the flexible tubing that brought gas to the intake; then, the gas container is put on a weighing scale; and an alternate – slightly awkward – method of filling the cylindrical container behind the cockpit.

Above: Test pilot Fay climbing out of the ski-equipped Bf 109E-8. The wartime German censor carefully cropped the photo to avoid showing the actual ski-undercarriage here.
H Fay

Right: The Bf 109E-8 with ski-undercarriage at Gardemoen airfield, Norway, in the winter 1940-41.

after 60 flights and certain modifications did the gondola-cannon installation prove satisfactory. Further trials were carried out with *WN* 13149, while between 11 and 16 May, 1942, four Bf 109Gs were equipped with the MG 151/20 conversion kit and sent to the front for operational evaluation. Not all pilots liked the gondolas. In 1974 Gunther Rall, who survived the war as a major with 275 accredited victories, remembered:

'We had those gondolas but when turning with a high G-factor the metallic cartridge links often gave way and the cannon jammed. They also caused additional drag, so I said "Get them off".'

A lesser-known activity of the Messerschmitt works was the development of variable propeller pitch mechanisms for engines of different horse-power. The series ran from Me P1 to Me P7; the last named being much used before the war in the Bf 108. It could run for 200 hours without servicing, and was one of the lightest and simplest mechanisms of its kind. It was manufactured by Messerschmitt but took wooden propeller blades supplied by Propellerwerk Gustav Schwarz GmbH of Berlin-Waidmannslust. Intended for much higher power was the Me P6. One of these was modified so that negative pitch could be used to obtain reverse thrust. It was installed in Bf 109-F4, *WN* 70003 and flown for 30 hours at Rechlin, during which about 100 braked landings were made. The trials ran under Erprobungs Nr 2601, and on 12 October, 1942 the final report was issued. It was intended to develop the Me P6 so that ultimately it could be used for braking purposes after touchdown by multi-engined aircraft, and as an air brake for dive bombers. The first trials were made with a 'feeler' extending below the fuselage. As soon as this feeler contacted the ground, negative pitch was automatically selected. However, too many malfunctions were experienced, and the feeler idea was discarded. Tests showed a markedly reduced roll-out after touchdown. If negative pitch was selected at the moment of touching down, roll-out distances of 135 to 150 metres were obtained. If however negative pitch was selected before touchdown, at a height of approximately 0.5 metres, then the distance was only 110-130 metres. Later on six Bf 109Gs were equipped with the special Me P6 at Wiener-Neustadt and tested by Erprobungskommando Lärz. Ultimately, the Me P6 'braking propeller' was used in variants of the Bf 109 such as G-2/U1, G-4/U1 and G-6/U1; as witnessed by Rechlin Erprobungsbericht Nr 136/43 gKdos – which in fact was the *Kennblatt* of the Bf 109G-1 with DB605A engine – issued on 8 March, 1943.

In early 1938 trials with 65-mm rockets had been initiated at Tarnewitz using a Bf 110. Report E6/1362/43 geh, issued by E'Stelle Tarnewitz on 19 May, 1943, constituted the manual for the Bf 109 F2 equipped with eight EG RZ65 underwing rocket launchers. Besides practice ammunition, two types of rocket could be used. AZ65 had an explosive charge of 130g which exploded on impact, but could only be used against ground targets. ZZ 1577 exploded on impact, or approximately four seconds after leaving the launcher tube, so could be used against ground or air targets, and had an explosive charge of 190g. The manual pointed out that due to the longer flight duration of the rocket compared to gun or cannon shells, and due to greater variations between flight trajectories caused by rocket propulsion, the aiming results were worse than with normal armament. The slightest inaccuracy in flying – slipping or skidding – produced even poorer results. The EG RZ65 was especially effective against enemy bomber formations. The manual specified two types of attack against such targets; both from a range of 1,000 metres. The first was from behind. Because the rocket lost five metres of height for every 100 metres flown, releasing the rockets had to be done while the Bf 109 was flying at a positive angle of attack of about 1.2 degrees. Aim had to be taken at the formation centre, not at individual bombers. This also applied to the second form of attack recommended – frontally. Using the EG RZ65 against small targets, or while shooting with large deflection, was not recommended.

During 1942 the Rheinmetall-Borsig firm developed a new type of 30-mm cannon, the MK 108, which was tested at Tarnewitz in 1943. The first 30 Bf 109G6-U4s to be equipped with two wing-mounted MK 108s were also tested at Tarnewitz. The aircraft were delivered there without cannon, and Report E6/1777/43 geh, dated 21 July, 1943 covered the trials. The cannon were supplied by DWM at Posen where series production was just beginning; while necessary parts were supplied by the Rheinmetall-Borsig firm of Berlin-Tegel. At the end of May nine cannons had been delivered but, when tested in a ground rig, showed so many defects that it was pointless mounting them in the 109s. The cannons were sent back to the manufacturer who, in mid-June, sent a new batch of 24. This second batch was considerably better and could be installed in the aircraft. Never-

In the summer of 1943 a wooden wing for the Bf 109 was experimentally built by Wolf Hirth GmbH. Here it can be seen aboard a lorry in August 1943 prior to delivery to the Luftwaffe.

theless, several misfirings still occurred, and cannon often had to be dismounted and rectified on the ground. When the report was compiled only 10 Bf 109s were at Tarnewitz; the other 20 were still at Schwerin and Lärz. The most common faults were listed as;

* Failure to fire due to firing pin striking cap off-centre
* Shells failing to eject due to too-tight fit
* Faults in shell feed due to manufacturer's errors
* Cracks in cannon mantle. Cured by welding on strengthening; but after firing 200 rounds, ten cannon showed cracks of such magnitude that weapons became useless.
* Fracture of small items.

At the end of 1943 Haupt-Ing Volak of the RLM and Dipl Ing Schneider of the E'Stelle Rechlin visited JG1 in Holland to investigate the problem of icing on the inside of the cockpit of Bf 109G-5s and G-6s, and Focke-Wulf Fw 190s. Their report was compiled at Rechlin on 20 December, 1943. While climbing or flying horizontally at height, the G-5s and G-6s cockpits often started icing up, starting at the rear and eventually covering the whole canopy interior – except the front armoured window – with ice. The reason was found to be a lack of air circulation inside the insulated cabin. This was often caused by pilots not pressurising the cabin – either because they did not like the noise made by

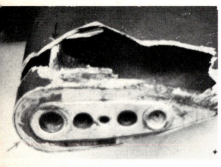

Top: The right tailplane of a factory-fresh Bf 109G-6, Wk Nr 165689, showing how the total wooden covering had become unglued.

Above: Bf 109, Wk Nr 166261, the elevator of which came loose from the hinge-carrying spar.

the compressor; or simply because no pressure was developed anyway, due to insulation leakage.

As the war progressed the scarcity of aluminium forced the German aircraft industry to revert to the use of wood. Several variants of Bf 109G had wooden tailplanes, but these caused many complaints. On 22 August, 1944, I./JG3 sent a complaint to Rechlin concerning Bf 109 wooden tailplanes and immediately five of the unit's fighters were examined by Hauptmann Lichtenecker from Rechlin. The resulting report, dated 22 September, 1944, also covered deficiencies in wood items and assemblies in the Bf 110, Junkers Ju 352, and Kalkert Ka 430, Three G-6s were found to be defective; *WN* 166261 had been standing in the open since 21 July, 1944 and flown a total of 23 hours 30 minutes. The right elevator showed three cracks of 15 millimetres length, cracks in the front spar, and a poor protective layer on the hinge-carrying spar; *WN* 165485, with a total flying time of three hours, and no exposure to the elements, showed cracks near the right elevator hinge; while *WN* 165689, fresh from the factory, showed a 60mm long crack in its right elevator, and ungluing of the rear spar of the right tailplane. This tailplane was taken off and sent to Rechlin for closer examination. The report stated that use of this tailplane would have caused an accident. It went on to state that neither the gluing, nor the protection of the wood, nor the craftsmanship was done in an expert manner. 'In view of such faulty manufacture the further use of wooden tailplanes must be questioned; the safety of the Bf 109 is highly endangered.' The reason for such poor manufacturing was the fact that the small woodworking firms that supplied the tailplanes to Messerschmitt simply did not have labour or staff with adequate experience in wood-working. Quite often foreign workers had to be employed. Some came to work in Germany voluntarily, but many had been forced to do so – sabotage was a tempting way of 'getting even.'

One of the many independent – unconnected with any university – aviation research facilities in Germany, in which some research on the Bf 109 was done, was the 'Ernst Udet' German Gliding Research Facility, temporarily situated at Ainring airfield, near Bad Reichenhall. This was also the nearest airfield to the Salzberg, Hitler's favourite haunt, and as such widely used by courier aircraft. Its history goes back to November 1924, when the Rhön-Rossitten-Gesellschaft e. V was founded to further gliding flight. It was named after the two main German gliding centres, and in 1925 its research institute took up its activities, mainly at the Wasserkuppe and Darmstadt. With the Nazi reorganisation

of aviation in Germany in 1933, the institute was renamed as the German Research Institute for Gliding, and placed under the jurisdiction of the German Air Sports Association. Soon after, however, it was transferred to the RLM, like all other independent aviation research facilities, and from then on was known as the Deutsche Forschungsanstalt für Segelflug (DFS) and located at the Darmstadt-Griesheim airfield. As soon as war broke out it was transferred to Brunswick and had to take on a wide range of research, some of which had no relation to gliding whatsoever. In the summer of 1940 it was transferred yet again, this time to Ainring airfield; and after the death of Ernst Udet on 17 November, 1941, the head of DFS, Prof Dr phil Dr Ing E.h. Walter Georgii, obtained permission to add Udet's name to that of DFS, in recognition of Udet's many services to the facility.

Among the trials and tests performed by the DFS were those investigating the possibilities of various *Mistel-Anordnungen* – pick-a-back combinations – some involving Bf 109s. A report dated 17 June, 1943, for example, gave its findings on a Junkers Ju 88A-4 and Bf 109F duo. In this example the Ju 88 was used as an unmanned bomber and the combination steered by the Bf 109 pilot only. In this manner it was possible to fly $3\frac{1}{2}$ tons of explosive over a range of 1,500km. The DFS had by then already tried a combination of a Me 328 with a Dornier Do 217, in which the Do 217 was used to fly the Me 328 glider-fighter above an enemy bomber formation. This proposal was dropped when it was decided to fit the Me 328 with two Argus As 014 pulse-jet engines. However, high hopes were placed in the Bf 109-Ju 88 combination, which acquired the name *Mistel* – Mistletoe – especially when the Ju 88 was equipped with a hollow charge warhead in its nose. Some *Mistels* were used against the Allied invasion fleet, and later against bridges over the River Oder captured by the Red Army, but no spectacular effect was ever achieved. Another pick-a-back combination – sometimes known as *Vater und Sohn* (Father and Son) – was a Bf 109E mounted on a DFS 230 transport glider, about which a report was compiled on 9 January, 1944. Formerly DFS 230s had been towed by a Klemm Kl 35 in this manner, also by a Focke-Wulf Fw 56. A new undercarriage had to be designed for the DFS 230, able to stand the stresses imposed by the weight of the Bf 109, especially when landing. DFS 230, D-14-884 was duly equipped with an undercarriage transmitting the weight of the Bf 109 directly to the wheels of the glider, which had been cannibalised from a Junkers W34.

The Bf 109 was fitted with supporting pads just forward of the wheels, and also near the

Left: PICK-A-BACK. D 14-884, a DFS 230, being 'towed' in pick-a-back fashion by a Bf 109E, June 1943. After release the glider – initially – tended to strike the Bf 109s under-fuselage.

Below left: Trajectories of the shells and bullets from the Bf 109's fuselage M-17; the engine MG 151/20; and the gondola MG 151/20 for comparison.

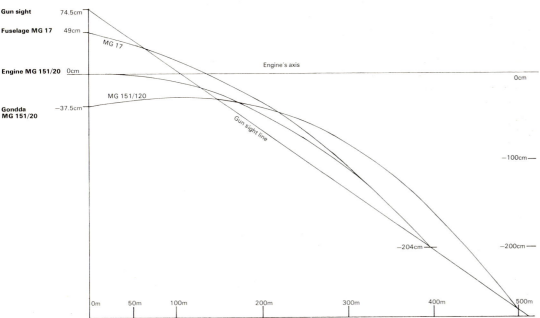

main spar-fuselage anchorage point. The DFS 230 was fitted with the necessary supporting struts. At first it was thought that Ainring airfield would not be big enough to carry out the tests safely, and it was decided to transfer them to Hörsching, near Linz. There the first tests were made on 21 June, 1943 which immediately made it clear that Ainring would be adequate, and the whole trial was re-transferred back to Ainring. It proved necessary to alter the support struts of the glider, as the latter usually struck the underside of the Bf 109 after release. A new system was installed on DFS 230, D-IEXX and on 16 July the trials were resumed. Again, the glider pitched upwards on release and hit the Bf 109. A special dive brake was therefore fitted on the glider, and the tests were finally completed to the satisfaction of the pilots involved – Flugkapitän Ing Zitter, Flugzeugführer Opitz, and Flugzeugführer Schieferstein. The DFS 230/Bf 109E combination resulted in perfect handling characteristics both in flight and on take-off and landing. It was controllable when using either the DFS 230s or the Bf 109s controls. When the controls of both were used in unison, overall control was extremely effective. It was possible to separate in flight, or to land while still coupled. The report ended by stating that further tests were being prepared whereby the control movements of the Bf 109 would be transferred to those of the DFS 230, and that no difficulties were expected.

An Emil called Mike

Early in 1941 a Japanese military mission made arrangements with Messerschmitt to build the Bf 109 under licence in Japan. After Messerschmitt's test pilot Willy Stör had demonstrated a Bf 109 and Bf 110 before the commission at Regensburg, he was asked to go to Japan to help supervise the assembly, do the test flying, and then help to train Japanese pilots. Stör left Germany on 4 May, 1941 and, travelling through Russia with his mechanic Herbert Kaden, he reached Tokio, where he was greeted by Wolfgang von Gronau – famous for his long distance flights with Dornier-Wal – and Heinkel's chief test pilot, Gerhard Nitschke. Stör took up residence at Gifa, where the Kawasaki Kokuki Kogyo KK works were situated, and where in the meantime three Bf 109E-3s and a Fieseler Storch had arrived. In October 1941 Stör's mission was completed but von Gronau kept him in Japan as adviser, and he often went to the Japanese testing centre at Tatshikawa to fly and give his opinion on various aircraft. By then the plan to licence-build Bf 109s in Japan had been dropped because of difficulties arising from the Allied blockade.

AN EMIL CALLED MIKE
Willy Stör with a
Japanese test pilot in front
of a Bf 109E, at Kawasaki
Kokuki Kogyo airfield, Gifu.

Stör was anxious to return to Germany, and on 18 April, 1942 was aboard a blockade-runner in the port of Yokohama when the ship was fired on by one of Jimmy Doolittle's 16 NA Mitchell B-25s which had taken off from *USS Hornet*. Another surprise came in the form of a telegram, ordering him to stay in Japan to direct the planned licence-construction of the Me 410 in Japan. A blockade-runner succeeded in bringing a Me 210 to Kobe, where it was assembled, though with difficulty because a second ship bringing the necessary blueprints had been sunk. The construction was planned at Kobe, but nothing came of it in the event. Due to the circumstances of the war Stör remained in Japan until February 1947, when an American troop carrier finally brought him back to Germany. Allied aircrews flying in the Pacific repeatedly reported sighting German aircraft types, and therefore it was – erroneously – believed that Japan was licence-building these and operating them. Though only three Bf 109Es were actually tested in Japan, the type was often reported, and given the code name Mike . . . it was an Emil called Mike.

Flying the Bf109

A captured Bf 109E in Paris,
21 November, 1939, in the
Place de la Concorde.

The war was only weeks old when, on 22 November, 1939, no less than three Bf 109s fell into the hands of the French; two of them wholly intact. One made a wheels-up landing near Puttelange, 15km south-east of Luxemburg city, alongside the cross-roads between Route-Nationale 56 and the road to Remeringles-Puttelange. Its pilot, a *Leutnant* of I./JG 76 (which unit became II./JG 54 in 1940), was captured and taken to the headquarters of the 41e Regiment de Mitrailleurs d'Infantrie Coloniale which guarded that section of the Maginot Line. The aircraft, Bf 109E, *WN* 1251, was exhibited in January 1940 on the Avenue des Champs Elysées; the proceeds of the display going to 'Pour ceux de l'escadrille' – a charity organisation of the French Air Force. A second Bf 109 made a normal landing at the Strasbourg-Neuhof aerodrome, south of Strasbourg. Its pilot, Vienna-born Oberfeldwebel Herfried Kloimüller of II./JG 51, was made prisoner, and the French air force decided to evaluate the machine. Capitaine Rozanoff of GC II/4, the experienced test pilot who had already flown a Bf 109 in Spain in February 1938, was detailed to fly the aircraft to the Centre d'Essais du Materiel Aerien (CEMA) at Orleans-Bricy aerodrome. He took off from Strasbourg on 28 November, escorted by Lieutenant Vinçotte and Adjutant Baptizet, also of II/4 and each flying a Curtiss 75. Flying very low in close formation at high speed, they reached Toul airfield where Rozanoff wanted to show the Messerschmitt to the pilots of GC II/5. Vinçotte broke away left, Baptizet to the right, but then Rozanoff decided to do a roll . . . Baptizet remembered, 'I gave full throttle and climbed. It was then that a grey mass loomed up in front of me; the 109, flying inverted!' Rozanoff was later to record,' Baptizet, flying very close, literally chewed away my tail with his propeller. I had to leave the stricken aircraft and jump by parachute.'

Luckily, the French had a second intact Bf 109. It was *WN* 1304, landed by a *Feldwebel* of I./JG 76, a veteran of the Legion Condor, at Woerth, Bas-Rhin, 40km north of Strasbourg. This 109E arrived at Orléans-Bricy on 6 December and due to bad weather made only seven flights, totalling five hours, before the end of the month. CEMA distributed 40 copies of its evaluation report, Rapport d'essai 403/S/SD. This preliminary report confirmed the performances claimed by the Germans, amongst other things a maximum speed of approximately 570km/hr at 5,000metres, but stated that while it was perfectly possible to aim correctly while diving, accurate firing was difficult while climbing. As the engine's torque was poorly compensated for, it was difficult for the Bf 109 to turn right while climbing. The report ended by advising pilots attacked by a Bf 109, or wanting to get away after an attack, to make a climbing turn to starboard. The final report by CEMA was issued on 30 March, 1940, numbered 291 S/SD. In the meantime, in his letter of 23 January, 1940, General Vuillemin, commander of the French air force, had asked for the Bf 109 to be tested against the Dewoitine D 520; while General d'Harcourt, Inspector-General of Fighters, in a letter dated March 25th, requested a comparison test with the Bloch 152 as well. The CEMA drew up a programme of such tests, not only with those two fighters but also with the Bloch 174 and Potez 63-11 reconnaissance and observation aircraft. At the end of March the Bf 109 was delivered to CEMA and a 35-mm Debrie cine camera gun was installed. As bad weather hindered the evaluation tests, the aircraft was taken from Orléans-Bricy to Marignane, near Marseille, where the tests were flown between 1 April and 21 April, 1940. On 27 April the CEMA issued its report, which stated that though the Bf 109 had a superior performance to the two French fighters, this did not give it complete superiority in aerial combat, and the that French fighters could oppose a Bf 109 with confidence. The Bloch 174 and Potez 63-11 also stood a good chance against the Messerschmitt; the Bloch through its speed, almost equal to that of the Bf 109; the Potez through its good manoeuvrability. The French, having extracted everything they wanted to know about the type, then handed over the aircraft to the RAF.

The Bf 109 was flown to RAF Boscombe Down on 4 May, 1940, where it was appraised by the Aircraft and Armament Experimental Establishment (A & AEE); then later flown to the Royal Aircraft Establishment (RAE) at Farnborough for handling trials, and allocated the serial number AE479. The results of the RAE's evaluation were discussed on Thursday, 9 March, 1944 at a meeting of the Royal Aeronautical Society in London, at which M B Morgan and R Smelt of the RAE lectured on 'The aerodynamic features of German aircraft.' About the Bf 109E they had this to say:
Take-off: This is best done with the flaps at 20 degrees. The throttle can be opened very quickly without fear of choking the engine. Acceleration is good, and there is little tendency to swing or bucket. The stick must be held hard forward to get the tail up. It is advisable to let the aeroplane fly itself off since, if pulled off too soon, the left wing will not lift, and on applying aileron the wing lifts and falls again, with the ailerons snatching a little. If no attempt is made to pull the aeroplane off quickly, the take-off is quite straightforward. Take-off run is short, and initial climb good.

Approach: Stalling speeds on the glide are 75mph flaps up, and 61mph flaps down. Lowering the flaps makes the ailerons feel heavier and slightly less effective, and causes a marked nose-down pitching moment, readily corrected owing to the juxtaposition of trim and flap operating wheels. If the engine is opened up to simulate a baulked landing with flaps and undercarriage down, the aeroplane becomes tail-heavy but can easily be held with one hand while trim is adjusted. Normal approach speed is 90mph. At speeds above 100mph the pilot has the impression of diving, and below 80mph one of sinking. At 90mph the glide path is reasonably steep and the view fairly good. Longitudinally the aeroplane is markedly stable, and the elevator heavier and more responsive than is usual in single-seater fighters. These features add considerably to the ease of approach. Aileron effectiveness is adequate; the rudder is sluggish for small movements.

Landing: This is more difficult than on the Hurricane 1 or Spitfire 1. Owing to the high ground attitude, the aeroplane must be rotated through a large angle before touchdown, and this requires a fair amount of skill. If a wheel landing is done the left wing tends to drop just before touchdown, and if the ailerons are used to lift it, they snatch, causing over-correction. The brakes can be applied immediately after touchdown without fear of lifting the tail. The ground run is short, with no tendency to swing. View during hold-off and ground run is very poor, and landing at night would not be easy.

Taxying: The aircraft can be taxied fast without danger of bucketing, but it is difficult to turn quickly; an unusually large amount of throttle is needed, in conjunction with harsh braking, when manoeuvring in a confined space. The brakes are foot-operated, and pilots expressed a strong preference for the hand operation system to which htey are more accustomed.

Lateral trim: There is no pronounced change of lateral trim with speed or throttle setting provided that care is taken to fly with no sideslip.

Directional trim: Absence of rudder trimmer is a bad feature, although at low speeds the practical consequences are not so alarming as the curves might suggest, since the rudder is fairly light on the climb. At high speeds, however, the pilot is seriously inconvenienced, as above 300mph about $2\frac{1}{2}°$ of port rudder are needed for flight with no sideslip and a very heavy foot load is needed to keep this on. In consequence the pilot's left foot becomes tired, and this affects his ability to put on left rudder in order to assist a turn to port. Hence at high speeds the Me 109E turns far more readily to the right than to the left.

Longitudinal trim: Five three-quarter turns of a 11.7in diameter wheel on the pilot's left are needed to move the adjustable tailplane through its full 12-degrees range. The wheel rotation is in the natural sense. Tailplane and elevator angles to trim were neasured at various speeds in various conditions; the elevator angles were corrected to constant tail setting. The aeroplane is statically stable both stick fixed and stick free.

'One control' tests, flat turns, sideslips: The aeroplane was trimmed to fly straight and level at 230mph at 10,000 feet. In this condition the aeroplane is not in trim directionally and a slight pressure is needed on the left rudder pedal to prevent sideslip. This influences the results of the following tests:

a *Ailerons fixed central.* On suddenly applying half-rudder the nose swings through about eight degrees and the aeroplane banks about five degrees with the nose pitching down a little. On releasing the rudder it returns to central, and the aeroplane does a slowly damped oscillation in yaw and roll. The right wing then slowly falls. Good banked turns can be done in either direction on rudder alone, with little sideslip if the rudder is used gently. Release of the rudder in a steady 30-degree banked turn in either direction results in the left wing slowly rising.

Bf 109E (Wk Nr 1304) of I./JG 76 undergoing evaluation by the French CEMA at Orléans-Bricy, and marked with French roundels over its German insignia. Note cine-camera (French) under wing. Along the leading edge of the wing was the inscription, 'Ne pas pousser ici' – Don't push here.

b *Rudder fixed central.* Abrupt displacement of the ailerons gives bank with no appreciable opposite yaw. On releasing the stick it returns smartly to central with no oscillation. If the ailerons are released in a 30-degree banked turn, it is impossible to assess the spiral stability, since whether the wing slowly comes up or goes down depends critically on the precise position of the rudder. Excellent banked turns can be done in either direction on ailerons alone. There is very little sideslip on entry or recovery, even if the ailerons are used very harshly. In the turn there is no appreciable sideslip.

c *Steady flat turn.* Only half-rudder was used during this test. Full rudder can be applied with a very heavy foot load, but the nose-down pitching movement due to sideslip requires a quite excessive pull on the stick to keep the nose up. When flat turning steadily with half-rudder, wings level, about half opposite aileron is needed. The speed falls from 230mph to 175mph, rate of flat turn is about 110.

d *Steady sideslip when gliding.* Gliding at 100mph with flaps and undercarriage up the maximum angle of bank in a straight sideslip is about five degrees. About 1/4 opposite aileron is needed in conjunction with full rudder. The aeroplane is fairly nose-heavy, vibrates and is a little unsteady. On release of all three controls the wing comes up quickly and the aeroplane glides steadily at the trimmed speed. With flaps and undercarriage down, gliding at 90mph, the maximum angle of bank is again five degrees 1/5 opposite aileron being needed with full rudder. The nose-down pitching movement is not so pronounced as before, and vibration is still present. Behaviour on releasing the control is similar to that with flaps up.

Stalling test. The aeroplane was equipped with a 60 foot trailing static head and a swivelling pitot head. Although, as may be imagined, operation of a trailing static from a single-seater with a rather cramped cockpit is a difficult job, the pilot brought back the following results:

Lowering the ailerons and flaps thus increases C_L max by 0.5. This is roughly the value which would be expected from the installation.

Behaviour at the stall. The aeroplane was put through the full official tests. The results may be summarised by saying that the stalling behaviour, flaps up and down, is excellent. Both rudder and ailerons are effective right down to the stall, which is very gentle, the wing only falling about 10 degrees and the nose falling with it. There is no tendency to spin. With flaps up the ailerons snatch while the slots are opening, and there is a buffeting on the ailerons as the stall is approached. With flaps down there is no aileron snatch as the slots open, and no pre-stall aileron buffeting. There is thus no warning of the stall, flaps down. From the safety viewpoint this is the sole adverse stalling feature; it is largely offset by the innocuous behaviour at the stall and by the very high degree of fore and aft stability on the approach glide.

Safety in the dive. During a dive at 400mph all three controls were in turn displaced slightly and released. No vibration, flutter or snaking developed. If the elevator is trimmed for level flight at full throttle, a large push is needed to hold in the dive, and there is a temptation to trim in. If, in fact, the aeroplane is trimmed into the dive, recovery is difficult unless the trimmer is wound back owing to the excessive heaviness of the elevator.

Ailerons. At low speeds the aileron control is very good, there being a definite resistance to stick movement, while response is brisk. As speed is increased the ailerons become heavier, but response remains excellent. They are at their best between 150mph and 200mph, one pilot describing then as an 'ideal control' over this range. Above 200mph they start becoming unpleasantly heavy, and between 300mph and 400mph are termed 'solid' by the test pilots. A pilot exerting all his strength cannot apply more than one-fifth aileron at 400mph. Measurements of stick-top force when the pilot applied about one-fifth aileron in half a second and then held the ailerons steady, together with the corresponding time to 45 degrees bank, were made at various speeds. The results at 400mph are given below:

Max sideways force a pilot can apply conveniently to the Me 109 stick 40lb.
Corresponding stick displacement 1/5th
Time to 45-degree bank 4 seconds
Deduced balance factor Kb2 —0.145

Several points of interest emerge from these tests:

a Owing to the cramped Me 109 cockpit, a pilot can only apply about 40lb sideway force on the stick, as against 60lb or more possible if he had more room.

b The designer has also penalised himself

ness has disappeared. Between 200mph and 300mph the rudder is the lightest of the three controls for small movements, but at 300mph and above, absence of a rudder trimmer is severely felt, the force to prevent sideslip at 400mph being excessive.

Harmony: The controls are well harmonised between 150mph and 250mph. At lower speeds harmony is spoiled by the sluggishness of the rudder. At higher speeds elevator and ailerons are so heavy that the word 'harmony' is inappropriate.

Aerobatics: These are not easy. Loops must be started from about 280mph when the elevator is unduly heavy; there is a tendency for the slots to open at the top of the loop, resulting in aileron snatching and loss of direction. At speeds below 250mph the aeroplane can be rolled quite quickly, but in the final stages of the roll there is a strong tendency for the nose to fall, and the stick must be moved well back to keep the nose up. Upward rolls are difficult. Owing to elevator heaviness only a gentle pull-out from the dive is possible,

by the unusually small stick-top travel of four inches, giving a poor mechanical advantage between pilot and aileron.

c The time to 45-degrees bank of four seconds at 400mph, which is quite excessive for a fighter, classes the aeroplane immediately as very unmanoeuvrable in roll at high speeds.

Elevator. This is an exceptionally good control at low air speeds, being fairly heavy and not over-sensitive. Above 250mph, however, it becomes too heavy, so that manoeuvrability is seriously restricted. When diving at 400mph a pilot, pulling very hard, cannot put on enough 'g' to black himself out; stick force-'g' probably exceeds 20 lb/g in the dive.

Rudder. The rudder is light, but rather sluggish at low speeds. At 200mph the sluggish-

and considerable speed is lost before the upward roll can be started.

Fighting qualities: A series of mock dogfights with our own fighters brought out forcibly the good and bad points of the aeroplane. These may be summarised as follows:

a Good points;
  *High top speed and excellent rate of climb
  *Engine does not cut immediately under negative 'g'.
  *Good control at low speeds
  *Gentle stall, even under 'g'.
b Bad points;
  *Ailerons and elevator far too heavy at high speeds
  *Owing to high wing loading the aeroplane stalls readily under 'g' and has a relatively poor turning circle

*Absence of a rudder trimmer, curtailing ability to bank left in the dive
*Cockpit too cramped for comfort.

A few of these points may be enlarged upon. At full throttle at 12,000 feet the minimum radius of steady turn without height loss is about 890 feet in the case of the Me 109E, with its wing loading of 32lb/sq ft. The corresponding figure for a comparable fighter with a wing loading of 25lb/sq ft, such as our Spitfire 1 or Hurricane 1, is about 690 feet. Although the more heavily loaded fighter is thus at a considerable disadvantage, it is important to bear in mind that these minimum radii of turn are obtained by going as near to the stall as possible. In this respect the Me 109E scores by its excellent control near the stall and innocuous behaviour at the stall, giving the pilot confidence to get the last ounce out of his aeroplane's turning performance.

The extremely bad manoeuvrability of the Me 109E at high air speeds quickly became known to our pilots. On several occasions a Me 109E was coaxed to self-destruction when on the tail of a Hurricane or Spitfire at moderate altitude. Our pilot would do a half-roll and a quick pull-out from the subsequent steep dive. In the excitement of the moment the Me 109E pilot would follow, only to find that he had insufficient height for recovery owing to his heavy elevator, and would go straight into the ground without a shot being fired.

Pilots' verbatim impressions of some features are of interest. For example, the DB 601 engine came in for much favourable comment from the viewpoint of response to throttle and insusceptability to sudden negative 'g'; while the throttle arrangements were described as 'marvellously simple, there being just one lever with no gate or over-ride to worry about.' Surprisingly though, the manual

Below: 'AUFSTEIGEN' – take-off; a Bf 109G-2 at the point of getting airborne. Probably a training machine from one of the 'Jagd-fliegerschulen (Fighter Pilots' Schools)./Bundesarchive

Bottom: This Bf 109E-4/Trop of I./JG 27 crashed and partly burned at Graz airfield (now in Austria), 6 April, 1941. Original photo taken by the Bildstelle Fliegerhorst Graz (Graz airfield Photo Section.)

operation of flaps and tail setting were also liked; 'they are easy to operate, and being manual are not likely to go wrong'; juxtaposition of the flap and tail actuating wheels is an excellent feature.'

Performance by 1940 standards was good. When put into a full throttle climb at low air speeds, the aeroplane climbed at a very steep angle, and our fighters used to have difficulty in keeping their sights on the enemy even when at such a height that their rates of climb were comparable. This steep climb at low air speed was one of the standard evasion manoeuvres used by the German pilots. Another was to push the stick forward abruptly and bunt into a dive with considerable negative 'g'. The importance of arranging that the engine should not cut under these circumstances cannot be over-stressed. Speed is picked up quickly in a dive, and if being attacked by an aeroplane of slightly inferior level performance, this feature can be used with advantage to get out of range. There is no doubt that in the autumn of 1940 the Me 109E in spite of its faults, was a doughty opponent to set against our own equipment.'

Selected comments from the men who flew and fought in the Bf 109E make interesting footnotes to the foregoing 'enemy' opinions: *Hauptmann Günther Schack, 174 victories;* 'In March 1941, as a Gefreiter, I joined

Jagdgeschwader Mölders, JG 51, stationed at St Omer, France. By then I had only taken off with the 109 straight into wind, and never from a concrete runway. On 4 April, during a cross-wind take-off on the concrete runway, the 109 swung so much to the left that I feared it would crash into some other machines parked along the edge of the field. I closed the throttle and my first crash began. The machine swung left even more, the left undercarriage-leg broke, and the 109 dropped on its left wing. This happed to me twice – second time on 10 April – and my future as a fighter pilot seemed sealed . . . In all, I was shot down 15 times . . . on one occasion I saw the right wing of my 109 flying right alongside me! During an attack on a bomber formation I was hit by an enemy fighter, right in one of the main spar attachment lugs. Luckily, I was over 2,000 metres high, but even then I only succeeded in getting out of the crazily-spinning machine close to the ground. I crashed against the tailplane, and for the next two weeks I could only walk bent in two . . .'

Major Günther Rall, 275 victories:
'The 109? That was a dream, the non plus ultra. Just like the F-14 today. Of course, everyone wanted to fly it as soon as possible. I was very proud when I converted to it.'

Generalleutnant Werner Junck, Inspector of Fighters, 1939:
'The 109 had a big drawback, which I didn't like from the start. It was that rackety – I always said rackety – undercarriage; that negative, against-the-rules-of-statics undercarriage that allowed the machine to swing away.'

Top and above: About to over-shoot into the trees beyond, this Bf 109E-1 pilot chose to do a violent ground-loop. It resulted in the right undercarriage leg being torn off completely./ *W Schäfer*

Below : FROM RUSSIA WITH HATE. A happy pilot of III./JG 54 viewing the damage in the tail section of his Bf 109F-2 after a near-miss from Soviet anti-aircraft guns./ *Bundesarchiv*

Top: Ground collision between two Bf 109G-2s of III./JG 54./*A Weise*

Above: Despite the already cramped cockpit, two-seat versions of the fighter were evolved. Two Bf 109G-12 versions at Pau, France in 1944. The nearest is 'Yellow 27' – formerly BJ+DZ – of 2./JG 101./*A Weise*

Left: Refuelling 'Yellow 27'. The Bf 109G-12 two-seat variant was delivered to several 'Jagdfliegerschulen' as conversion trainers in late 1943; and in the following year also used by most training 'Geschwadern'./*A Weise*

145

Above: A 'Bf 109' which never flew – a decoy wood-and-canvas 'fighter' to fool marauding Allied fighters./*Bundesarchiv*

Right: Closing in . . .

Facing page: The Bf 109's nose . . . /
Bundesarchiv (*all four*)

146

Bf 109B-1   Bf 109E-1

Bf 109F-0   Bf 109G-4.

Appraisal

RUDOLF SINNER

'As long as the war between fighter and fighter assumed priority for us during the 1939 – 41/42 period, the 109 proved itself to be an excellent and more or less universal fighter, superior to any Allied fighter of the time, except perhaps the Spitfire. It was also useful for fighting the small and poorly defended bomber formations that appeared sporadically at the period. However, it rapidly lost its high status as a standard fighter when more and more compact, heavily-defended and protected enemy bomber units came to be used. Due to its vulnerability to enemy fire, and its weak armament for such targets, it proved to be poorly suited for an attack under fire from the defensive armament of close-flying bomber formations. Trying to improve the Bf 109Gs armament by so-called gondola cannon resulted in poorer handling qualities, and therefore the aircraft became inferior in combat with enemy fighters. To my mind – without that additional armament – the 109 remained superior to the Russian YAK 9 until the end of the war; more or less useful in battle with the Mustang; but inferior in certain important aspects to the Spitfire and Tempest.

'The devastating losses suffered by the 109 during the last years of the war should not be attributed so much to superiority of enemy fighters, as is generally assumed. They were caused by a combination of various circumstances. First, German fighters then always faced an overwhelming number of enemy fighters. Their assigned task required a consistent concentration against enemy bombers, which usually kept them from any offensive operations against enemy fighters. Concentrating on the bombers forced them to use a number of technical and tactical measures which made it easier for enemy fighters to shoot them down with less risk to themselves. Formating, climbing, approach and attack in close formation, often with aircraft hindered and slowed by cannon gondolas or rockets; flying back after attacking the bombers, little fuel and no ammunition, often alone, damaged, possibly wounded; then having to find a bombed airfield, under enemy fighter assault; all this, and the storm attacks under massive fire from the bomber gaggles, caused heavy

148

losses – which could not be made good because scarcity of fuel allowed no further training of operationally fit replacements. In short, until 1941-42, the 109 gave us superiority in combat with enemy fighters universally. In fighting heavily defended targets in the air or on the ground, it rapidly proved less suited than other types of fighter which Germany was by then producing. A timely strengthening of the day-fighter arm with units equipped with other types (of fighter) and a simultaneous specialisation (of roles) would have been possible and expedient. For fighting against enemy fighters and fighter-bombers, the 109 remained useful until the end of the war, but was in no case a superior weapon. From 1942-43 there were types (of fighter) better suited for further development, and which were ready for use.'

Above left: TAKE-OFF. Bf 109Es of 7./JG 53 'Pik As' at Caffiers, 1940./A Weise

Far left: 'ALARMSTART'! Mechanics jump into action as the alert signal sounds . . . November 1939 scene.

Left: Helping the pilot into his parachute. The Hakenkreuz (swastika) on this Bf 109E overlapped the rudder; a practice officially discontinued in March 1940 though some aircraft still displayed the out-dated marking months later.

Below: BROTHERS IN DEATH. A Bf 109E-4 and a Hawker Hurricane lie together on a deserted beach; both victims of an aerial combat./G Rall

Left: Above the clouds, a 109E-4 patrolling./*M Villing*

Top right: The undercarriage . . . always, that undercarriage! A Bf 109E-3 with a bent left leg, after a Bumslandung (bumpy landing).

Centre right: UNDER THE ROMAN SUN. Ground crews relax in Italian sunshine near their 'charge', an oddly camouflaged Bf 109G-6/R3 belonging to the 'Gruppen' adjutant of JG 77, 1944./ *Bundesarchiv*

Bottom right: Undercarriage problems for the ground crew of this Bf 109E-1 of JG 331 (later JG 77) at Frankfurt-Oedheim airfield, 1939. The personal insigne on the nose of the aircraft is a cartoon boot./*W Schäfer*

Under New Management

Bf 109G-2 (Wk Nr 10639),
captured in Sicily, and in
1944 with No 1426 Flight,
RAF as RN 228./
Imperial War Museum

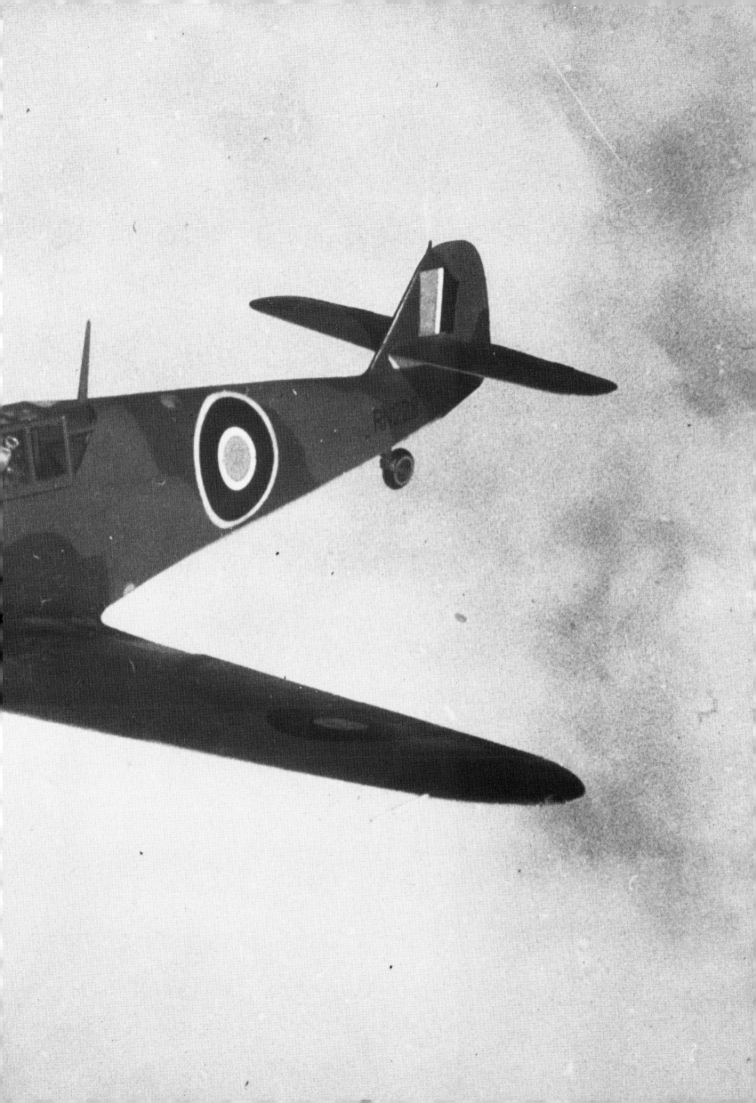

Above: The Bf 109F-1, flown by Rolf Pingel, 'Kommandeur' of I./JG 26, which was brought down virtually intact on 10 June, 1941 during a combat over St Margaret's Bay, near Dover, Kent. The 22 victory symbols were marked in scarlet on the bright yellow rudder. This aircraft was repaired and then test-flown as ES 906. Pingel had flown about 550 missions by that date, including sorties in Spain, where he had claimed an additional four victories./*Imperial War Museum*

Far left: Intact Bf 109G-6/R6 of II./JG 53, 'Pik As' on a Sicilian airfield, complete with underwing gondola cannons; alongside a Spitfire IX of the Desert Air Force./*Imperial War Museum*

Left: This Bf 109G-14/AS was captured at Stendahl, 50 km north of Magdeburg, by American troops. They also discovered a number of operational Me 262 jets of 3./JG 7, 'Nowotny'./*USAF*

Below left: Two American fighter pilots of the 9th Tactical Air Command get to 'close range' with a Bf 109G-10, abandoned on a French airfield, and look over its DB 605AS engine installation. Left is 1st Lt Charles Katzenmeyer of Vicksburg, Miss, and right, 1st Lt Zell Smith of Monroe, La., USA./*USAF*

Aftermath

Wilhelm Kellermeier, retired Treasurer of Duingen, a small village some 40km south of Hanover, did not know where his father lay buried. His mother had simply told him that her husband had fallen in June 1915, in the Vosges hills. Where he was buried was, apparently, unknown – until his son took a holiday trip through France in 1970 and finally located his father's grave. Fifty five years had passed, but the grave had been cared for by the Volksbund Deutsche Kriegs-gräberfürsorge – the German association which looked after the graves of every German fallen in battle.

This discovery served to intensify Kellermeier's long efforts to establish the identity of the fighter pilot who had crashed at Duingen during World War 2, but whose body had never been recovered. His son-in-law had personally seen how, on 20 February, 1944, a Bf 109G had been attacked by a P-47 Thunderbolt, and how the Bf 109 had dived straight into the ground after a short burst from the American fighter. The German pilot did not leave his aircraft, which crashed in a brook. At the spot where the aircraft had come down little was to be found; a dark pool in the brook, covered with oil, and some wreckage from the wings. A few days later, a Wehrmacht recovery/salvage party arrived, diverted the brook, and started to search – in the wrong spot, not believing what local inhabitants had told them. Finding nothing, the search was soon discontinued, and parts of the aircraft wing and tail were taken away.

Nothing more was done until 1964, when Wilhelm Kellermeier first heard about it and started his efforts to raise the wreck so that the pilot's identity could be established. This proved easier said than done as little help was forthcoming. At last, on 13 November, 1973, the wreck was salvaged, and the pilot's skeleton found. A few days later the pilot's identity was established as Feldwebel Gerhard Raimann; and on 19 November his remains were buried with full military honours at the Salzderhelden Soldiers' Cemetery. Raimann had belonged to 7./JG 54, and when his former *Staffelkapitän*, was located in Switzerland, the full story became clear. On the day

that Raimann crashed, 'Big Week' had started – a series of bombing attacks upon the German aircraft industry – and that day the American 8th Air Force despatched 16 combat Wings to attack 12 targets in Germany. One of these was against the Erla works near Leipzig, where the Bf 109 was being licence-built in large numbers.

One of the German fighter units to attack the American armada was 7./JG 54, based at Ludwigslust, in Schwerin, about halfway between Hamburg and Berlin. The *Staffelkapitän* was Hauptmann Rudolf Klemm, 42 victories, and now living in Basle, Switzerland. On 3 March, 1944 he wrote to Raimann's parents to tell them that their son was missing in action, '. . . the Gruppe took off to attack a US bomber unit, protected by numerous fighters, intending to bomb targets in central Germany. About 1300 hours we contacted the head of the enemy formation. Your son was flying next to me when I shot down an enemy bomber out of a mass formation of 60 aircraft. Your son also took part in two subsequent attacks needed to shoot down the enemy bomber. During the last attack your son was bounced by an enemy fighter. He probably didn't hear the warning I gave through the

radio, and I myself was at that moment in a disadvantageous situation so that I could not intervene in time. Your son's aircraft went into a vertical dive after a short burst from behind, and was trailing smoke as it disappeared in to the cloud cover below. Our hope that your son might have jumped by parachute and, being wounded, had been taken to a hospital, is unfortunately no longer possible. Regrettably, we must now presume that he died during the aerial combat from wounds. The actual position of the aircraft is unknown; a precise location could not be made because of the cloud, and because the combat took place at 6,000 metres. I understand the Osnabrück-Hanover area seems indicated. Searching continues in this area . . .'

A few days after Raimann's burial, it was discovered that his mother was still living in the German Democratic Republic, aged 77. She was invited to stay for some time in Duingen, and arrived there on 16 February, 1974. A short while later she stood by her son's grave, clutching a yellowing, tear-stained piece of paper – the letter written by her son's *Staffelkapitän*, Klemm, 30 years before. Until that moment it had been the last she had ever heard of her son . . .

Top left: It was necessary to dig to a depth of five metres.

Left: Feldwebel Gerhard Raimann, pictured here as an Unteroffizier (Uffz) – who was 'missing' for nearly 30 years.

Above left: Wilhelm Kellermeier (rt) at the spot where the remains of Raimann's Bf 109G were found; two bent propeller blades and a Rheinmetall-Borsig MG 131.

Top: The pilot's watch, after 29 years, still indicating the time of the crash – five minutes before two o'clock . . .

Above: TO THE FALLEN . . . the tombstone at the head of Gerhard Raimann's grave at the Soldiers' Cemetery, inscribed with the wrong date of death. Since this photo was taken, this date has been corrected to 20 February, 1944.

159

Acknowledgements

The author wishes to extend his grateful thanks for the help received while researching this book. Especially to the ladies: E. Gemählich, T. Grether, C. Hirth, M. Knoetzsch, G. Lusser and F. Schacker and the following Gentlemen: F. Bartsch, W. Batz, K. Beeken, H. Birkholz, C. Cain, G. Debrödy, A. de Heppes, J. Dillen, A. Döring, J. Ellingworth, W. Eisenlohr, W. Falck, H. Fay, A. Fischer, F. Fuchs, A. Galland, G. Ghergo, W. Gollwitzer, J. Goodwin, H. Greiner, G. Handrick, F. Haubner, H. Herb, D. Holeczy, H. Horber, W. Hörning, F. Jaenisch, W. Junck (+), W. Kellermeier, F. Kirch, A. Köhler, F. Kovacs, H. Kroschinski, E. Leykauf, S. Litjens, A. Maes, H. Meier, F. Morzik, E. Neumann, E. Obermaier, T. Olausson, R. Olejnik, K. Pfeifer, G. Rall, A. Remondino, W. Rethel, K. Riess, B. Robertson, R. Rombaut, R. Rothenfelder, O. Rumler, H. Sander, G. Schack, W. Schäfer, H. Schliephake, H. Schlötzer, K. Schnittke, H. Scholl, R. Sinner. W. Schroer, J. Thévoz, H. Thurnheer, G. Thyben, H. Trautloft, W. Unger, G. van Acker, M. Villing, W. Voigt, H. von Bülow, P. von Schalscha-Ehrenfeld, A. Weise, J. Wiese, B. Widfeldt, D. Wollmann, E. Wren and H. Wurster.
Also the following institutions:
Abteilung der Militärflugplätze, Dübendorf
Air Force Museum, Ohio
Air Historical Branch (RAF) London
Bundesarchiv, Koblenz and Freiburg
Deutsche Dienststelle (WASt) Berlin
Deutsches Museum, Munich
Gemeinschaft der Jagdflieger e.V., Lütjenburg
Imperial War Museum, London
Lufthansa, Cologne
Messerschmitt, Bölkow, Blohm GmbH, Ottobrunn
Musée de l'Air, Paris
Public Records Office, London
R.A.F. Museum, Hendon
Service Historique de l'Armée de l'Air, Vincennes
Staats- und Stadtbibliothek, Augsburg
Stadtarchiv, Augsburg
Stadtarchiv, Regensburg
Stadtbibliothek, Regensburg
Z.L.D.I., Munich
I also want to thank Mr Chris Wren for permission to reproduce some of his "Oddentifications", the Ministry of Defence, London for permission to use the wartime "Cummings" cartoons which are Crown Copyright, Coward, McCann and Geoghegan, Inc, New York for permission to quote from "Airpower" by A. Williams and Harcourt, Brace, Jovanovich, Inc, New York for permission to quote from the "Wartime Journals of Charles A. Lindbergh".